Imagine

Ideation Skills for
Improvement and Innovation Today

John Canfield

with Greg Smith

Black Lake Press
TELL YOUR STORY
BLACKLAKEPRESS.COM

Black Lake Press
TELL YOUR STORY
BLACKLAKEPRESS.COM

Cover design by Greg Smith of Black Lake Studio.

Published by Black Lake Press of Holland, Michigan. Black Lake Press is a division of Black Lake Studio, LLC. Direct inquiries to Black Lake Press at *www.blacklakepress.com.*

ISBN 978-0-9824446-7-2

Author's Note

*Dedicated to the thousands of my clients
who had the courage to wonder, change,
and improve their workplaces.*

The *Good Thinking Series', Part One: Think or Sink. A Parable of Collaboration,* was a story, a narrative, an easy read.

Part Two, *Collaborate,* and this book, *Imagine,* are instruction books, and hence more like recipe books or repair manuals. As such, I believe that the reader will benefit from completing the exercises and applying the tools and techniques immediately. Just reading the text will not provide the learning and benefit available from actually practicing with the tools and techniques using your own data, focused on your own issues, and seeing and applying your own results.

Table of Contents

Introduction

The *Good Thinking Series* is intended to help its readers significantly improve their organization's performance. The first book in the series is *Think or Sink: A Parable of Collaboration*. This book follows three leaders (a *competer*, an *accommodator*, and a *collaborator*) as they work to complete a major project. We learn about how these three leaders think and behave, how their supporting teams think and work for the team, and the likely business impact of these three leadership strategies.

The second book in the series is *Collaborate: Tools and Techniques for Better Meetings*. This book helps readers learn how to think, behave, and lead as a collaborator.

Both of the third and fourth *Good Thinking Series* books explain collaboration strategies designed to generate better ideas in specific areas of need:

	Tactical	Strategic
Improve **(Convergent)**	Process Improvement Skills	Strategic Planning
	Collaboration Skills	
Innovate **(Divergent)**	Creative Thinking Skills	Scenario Planning

This third book in the series, *Imagine:Ideation Skills for Improvement & Innovation Today,* helps leaders learn to understand and use specific idea-generating skills (Process Improvement Skills and Creative Thinking Skills) that help users generate tactical ideas for both improvement and innovation.

The fourth book in the *Good Thinking Series* is *Plan: Skills for Improvement & Innovation Tomorrow.* It helps leaders learn to understand and use specific idea-generating skills (Strategic Planning and Scenario Planning) that help users generate strategic ideas for both improvement and innovation.

The Importance of Ideas

Idea generating skills are crucial to an organization's success. They are the stepping stones to decisions and support. Implemented well, the ideas are transformed into improved business performance.

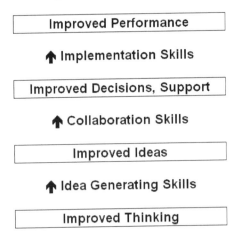

Considering that you cannot realize what you cannot

imagine, your ability to realize improved ideas can differentiate you from your competitors. Considering that you cannot will yourself a new idea, your ability to purposefully imagine improved ideas on demand can differentiate you from your competitors. The *Good Thinking Series* of books helps leaders and employees learn to think more effectively in a wide range of situations. The series helps leaders and employees learn to think more effectively on purpose, on demand.

Some Additional Helpful Ideas About Generating Ideas

Marvin Weisbord has developed a concept he calls *equifinality*. It describes a situation in which there is likely more than one way, one idea, that will support a given set of goals. There's more than one way to do things successfully. This takes the stress off finding *the* right answer. Rather, try to find three solutions to a problem. Then pick one and work hard to make it a success.

Joseph Juran, in *The Pareto Principle* (the "80/20" rule), argued that among many ideas, a few will provide dramatic results. This idea helps us target the significant few, and leave the trivial many until later. You don't need to have a long to do list in order to be successful. In fact, you don't want to: a long to do list is counter-productive to success.

Learning and using the approaches and techniques found in the *Good Thinking Series* is like taking ownership for the software on your computer, and not letting random programs confuse or derail your work efforts. The series is written to introduce the fundamental topics. There are many great resources to help you once you have actually started successfully. My main interest is helping the many company leaders and employees who have not yet started to make their thinking purposeful and effective. Either they've tried and failed, or they just have not found a resource to help them move from where they are and begin building momentum with their new thinking.

After decades of studying a wide variety of organizations around the world, I've come to the following conclusion: few of the many thousands of companies currently operating have shown that they have the thinking skills and discipline to successfully implement and maintain the benefits of the many improvement strategies available. I've written this series of books to help leaders begin or review a topic and then successfully implement the thinking and skills of productive collaboration and realize the benefits in their organization.

Resistant Leaders

Good Thinking Series, Part 3, Imagine: Ideation *Skills for Improvement and Innovation Today* is a book for beginners. Beginners who want to learn how to ideate, how to develop more ideas when they need them. This book is also for those who are not satisfied with their previous encounters with these two topics and want to begin again.

This book will address both process improvement skills (problem solving ideas for today) and creative thinking skills (innovative ideas for today). Business leaders have exercised these two skill sets with other methods for decades. With process improvement, many companies have relied on fire fighting to keep ahead of the curve while other companies like Toyota, for one, have learned to solve problems deliberately by using tools and techniques that guide a team's thinking to more quickly and accurately identify and eliminate the causes to problems.

With creativity, many companies have relied on Tom or Sally, the creative ones around this company, while other companies like Ideo, for one, have learned to come up with useful new ideas deliberately by using tools and techniques that guide a team's thinking to more quickly and productively identify and develop novel alternatives.

A significant bind may exist in some companies at this juncture, to rely on a less formal approach, or learn and use a more structured approach. "But we've always done it that way !" will be claimed in some companies for both problem solving and creativity. Arguments I've heard from reluctant problem solving students include "We haven't got time for this stuff...we've got problems to solve..things to get done!" Arguments I've heard from reluctant creative thinking students include "Creative process...oh...is an oxymoron. Please don't add any structure or method to our exclusive strength."

The tools and techniques in the *Good Thinking Series* are not intended to replace the less formal processes that work for companies. They complement them. I am certainly not suggesting companies stop doing what's working. I am suggesting that companies work hard to continue to improve on what is working to remain competitive. I am suggesting that companies using tools and techniques will very much broaden both the number of options they can generate, and the number of employees who can help in problem solving and creative work. A company's next improvements and innovations may be hiding at the boundaries of their comfort zone. The *Good Thinking Series* is one resource to help companies raise the bar.

"The exact contrary of what is generally believed is often the truth."—Jean de la Bruyère

1
Ideation—Restraining and Promoting Considerations

The Merriam-Webster dictionary defines *ideation* as, "The capacity for or the act of forming or entertaining ideas."

When we are on an idea search, we are on a scavenger hunt for alternatives. As the iceberg diagram below attempts to show, not all the ideas we'd like to consider are above water, on the table, available to be discussed.

Ideas:

Know - Share

water line

Know - Don't Share

Know - Forgot

New - Thought for the First Time Ever

In a team environment, the ideas we know and share (above the water line) are often politically correct. This is similar to "weather talk" in the Stage Theory of Team Development (the "form/storm/norm/perform" model that Bruce Tuckman first described in 1965). Below the water line, "under the table," are many ideas that we share in confidence. These ideas are deemed not so politically correct, even politically dangerous, and often introduced with words that hint at a deeper meaning: "Well, to tell the truth..." The ideas we forget can be retrieved if we're lucky to have notes and documents. The brand-new ideas can occur accidently while walking the dog, or generated deliberately with the tools from this *Good Thinking Series*, books 3 and 4, and many other resources.

This is just as true for individuals as it is among groups. The ideas we like and think of often are above the line. The ideas that we may know, but not share (even with ourselves), hide in our denial. It's easy to forget ideas. And of course the same idea-generating tools can help individuals come up with ideas on demand when they know how to—and want to.

Junk Drawer

Let's review an experience we've all likely had. I'll assume you have a junk drawer at home. In my many seminar presentations around the world, I have yet to find a modern culture that does not include junk drawers. The junk drawer is a drawer like no others anywhere in the house. It is full of all sorts of odds and ends. And, around the world, we all use it the same way: something is broken, you're hunting for a solution, and you head to the junk drawer. Most of the time, you don't know what you're looking for—other than a solution—but you go to the junk drawer because it's worked before. You open it, scan the objects inside, and *presto!*—some sort of arrangement of the drawer's items jumps out at you as an alternative solution for your problem. You retrieve it and go give it a try. My point is that this happens for all of us, and we've come to rely on it as a method. Given an assortment of seemingly random resources, your brain can make new combinations and end up with a useful alternative that you did not have before.

Part of our work is to get as many good ideas as possible to be part of our conversation by lowering the water line in the diagram above. I'd like a great junk drawer full of optional ideas each time I'm trying to select one to fulfill a need. People can also be like junk drawers. Some are full of lots of options—ideas galore to share. Others have only a few ideas, or the drawer is jammed shut—not open for business.

New Idea Constrainers

It's all well and good to tell someone that they should be a better problem solver, more creative, or a better planner, but there are a factors that limit our creativity, or our attempts to solve problems and plan effectively.

One has to do with our position, our paradigms, how we see things. It seems some people think that the way they see things is the way things are. *"My way or the highway,"* or *"Everyone's entitled to my opinion,"* or *"Look at these parade marchers: everyone but my son is out of step."*

You've probably been around people who think this way. What happens when you challenge their point of view? They think and act defensively. They likely perceive that you are attacking them, not just their idea. They think of their idea and themselves as one.

Alternatively a person can learn to think that the way they look at things is only a current alternative. We could adopt the attitude that there's always a better way to do or think about something. I can choose to see myself as being on a treasure hunt for better ideas, and not too picky about where these better ideas might come from. I get to decide which ideas I like best. I am not my idea. Another constraint is hunger—hunger for ideas. If people aren't hungry, they won't look.

"It is a universal truth that those who are not dissatisfied will never make any progress. Yet even if one feels dissatisfaction, it must not be diverted into complaining; it must be actively linked to improvement. In this sense, we can say that dissatisfaction is the mother of improvement. There are many examples of waste in the workplace, but not all waste is obvious. It often appears in the guise of useful work. We must see beneath the surface and grasp the essence. Never being content and always looking for ways to make things better are prime prerequisites for uncovering problems."

—Dr. Charles J. Robinson, *Continuous Improvement in Operations: a Systematic Approach to Waste Reduction*, Productivity Press, Portland, Oregon, 1991

When we observe and listen to the dissatisfied person, our challenge is to not take their observations personally. Their feedback may be useful, and our keeping an open mind to the information will most often serve us well.

Another constraint is fear of change. If I can accept that I need new products and services to be competitive, then I need to improve. To improve, I have to change, to start doing something new, and stop doing something old.

Ideally I want to change and improve faster than my competitors. I accept I need an effective process to do this.

Eight Ball

There is at least one more constraint: Some people, unfortunately, often pre-judge their own ideas and do not share them with others for a host of social reasons: fear of embarrassment, kidding, seeming stupid—all the usual stuff.

Please help your brain clear itself of old rusty dusty ideas by acknowledging, documenting, and sharing them as they come to your imagination. Do not prejudge. Some of those "bad ideas" are someone else's junk drawer, just what they need to complement what's already in their own junk drawer. They can feed off your ideas and together you can come up with some truly new combinations.

Consider someone playing with that classic toy, the old, fortune-telling Magic Eight Ball. You shake this sphere of truth and—*pop,* up comes an answer. A different answer appeared each time, like a real-time fortune cookie. Have you ever noticed that some people keep shaking the ball until they get the answer they want? "Will I be rich and famous?" "No" ...*shake shake...* "Not today" ...*shake shake...* "Most certainly." *Ah, we have a winner!* Let the new and possibly different and unexpected ideas be included in your junk drawer. You may find a very good use for then down the road.

New Idea Promoters

The first part of this is easy—reduce or eliminate the constraints. Work hard to lower the water line on the previous iceberg diagram.

In the case of people stuck on their positions, initiating dialogue is one strategy to develop the opportunity to see things differently. Dialogue is an interactive conversation or experience that generates new knowledge.

This conversation is much improved with the aid of visual and hands-on mark 'em up charts, diagrams, etc., that focus on the current reality to begin with, and then a preferred state. These tools provide the participants a chance to document what's really happening and to question whether the current picture is accurate. These tools then provide the participants a chance to document what they really would prefer.

Finally, the charts and diagrams also provide a neutral place for the participants to look and, importantly, break eye-to-eye contact. People are far more likely to move into an unproductive argument if they're making a lot of eye contact and intent on protecting their position and status. A quick example might be the difference in a traveling couple who is lost with a map and one without a map. Without the map, they just bicker. With the map, they say, "Let's see, where are we?"

In the case of reluctant change participants, it seems that it is in our genes to resist change. Driven by a vision, these steps often take quite a bit of personal courage. People unfamiliar with how to lead innovation do not like change, even though they say they might. People struggle with what to do next. Change, like good ideas, is often only appreciated after it is in place. Successful innovation must be led. Someone in the organization has got to grab the torch and move the troops to a new level of capability.

In the case of hunger, we get motivated when we notice a difference between what we want and what we've got. Scoreboards are helpful here with real, objective numbers reflecting actual performance against goals. And to raise the goals, find and visit another organization that is demonstrating what's possible, i.e. benchmark. These are great learning opportunities for leaders and employees, creating opportunities for them to realize, "Wow, we could do that!"

Ask the Expert

Dr. de Bono, author of *Serious Creativity, Six Thinking Hats, Lateral Thinking,* and many other books about thinking skills defines a productive thinker as:

- confident and competent about their own thinking, not arrogant.
- thinks of themselves as a thinker, not thinking of themselves as intelligent and has all the answers, always right
- always get better at this skill.
- not always need to be right, can see other people's points of view.
- willing to explore situations, not just defend their point of view.
- willing to look for alternatives and look beyond obvious alternatives.
- can assess priorities and can evaluate alternatives, can make decisions.
- use deliberate creative tools.
- uses Lateral Thinking to generate fresh ideas; not just waiting for an idea, as inspiration or chance has an ability to sit down and generate new ideas; good craftsman, know how to use tools.

Productive dialogue provides two significant benefits. One of the benefits of effective dialogue is to identify a variety of good alternatives. Another benefit takes advantage of the wonderful principle "People support what they create." It is the combination of good decisions

with good support that provides planning team decisions which generate significant business impact.

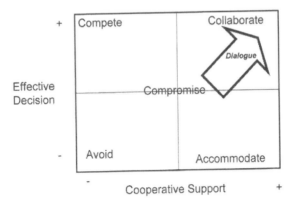

2
Successful Ideation— Fundamental Strategy

Thinking is a Skill

As we learned in *Good Thinking Series,* books 1 and 2, there is a difference between intelligence and thinking. Intelligence is our innate capability, what we're born with. Thinking, on the other hand, is how we learn to use our intelligence, and as such, is a skill. As a skill, like bowling, golfing, cooking, etc., it can be actively improved.

In one comparison, intelligence is the race car and it's finite mechanical capabilities, and thinking is the driver who can learn more and more about how to maximize the utility of the car. In a road racing betting opportunity, would you bet on the car or the driver?

Business Performance Improvement Requires Better Ideas, Better Thinking

Business performance improvement is built on a healthy sequence of improved decisions supported by the decision makers' organizations. Improved decisions come from improved thinking, the ability to solicit, consider, compare, and select good ideas.

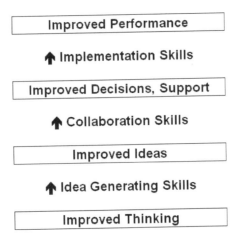

Effective process improvement is all about generating lots of good ideas about possible solutions, choosing and confirming the best, and implementing decisions that improve the target processes.

Effective creative thinking skills are all about generating lots of good ideas about possible new products and services that add to company revenues and profit.

In both cases the quality and quantity of good ideas depends on a person or a team's thinking skills.

Better Ideas From Better Thinking

To a layman's view, generating ideas is something that happens. It's a natural phenomenon.

Considering the physiological source of ideas, generating ideas is a neurological phenomenon. Over the past twenty years I have searched for helpful descriptions of this phenomenon. My favorite so far is from David Perkins (*Archimedes' Bathtub: The Art and Logic of Breakthrough Thinking;* Norton & Company, 2000). Perkins' five-step structure describes breakthrough thinking generating new ideas:

- **Long Search:** breakthrough thinking characteristically requires a long search
- **Little Apparent Progress:** a typical breakthrough arrives after little or no apparent progress.
- **Precipitating Event:** the typical breakthrough begins with a precipitating event. Sometimes external circumstances cue this moment.
- **Cognitive Snap:** the breakthrough comes rapidly, kind of falling into place, a cognitive snap. Not much time separates the precipitating event from the solution even if details remain to be checked.
- **Transformation:** the breakthrough transforms one's mental or physical world in a generative way.

I find this helpful. It tracks with my experience, individually and as a member of teams.

Without the aid of deliberate thinking skills, working randomly, not knowing any better, I start squinting my eyes and gazing off into space looking for new ideas. It doesn't work too effectively, so it takes quite a while, frustrating me with little progress. Then something happens—bordering on a miracle, depending on the significance of the need for the idea—and the idea snaps into my head like a road sign coming around a bend. Once I have the idea, I'm off to trying it on my need.

For example, I once lost my keys. I did not want to be late to an event so I was under pressure, so my amygdala (emotional decision making area of my brain) kicks in leaving me with emotional thinking and emotional choices: the cat took them, someone moved them (blame blame), I've lost them forever, etc.

So, to practice what I preach, as I could not admit that I lost my keys, I sat down to reduce my stress and engage my better thinking. Where in my day's process so far might I have left me keys?. So I imagined my day so far, and long story short, I remembered I took a walk in morning, then chose some clothes to give to the Goodwill store, and had put them in a bag, and *a ha!* The keys were in the pocket of the pants I had worn that morning and put into the bag.

The point of the story is to appreciate that the Perkins model is useful in considering how one organizes their thinking in trying to deliberately come up with useful ideas. In the lost keys case, the precipitating event was choosing to think about the losing of the keys as a process, think it through objectively, and *presto,* the keys were found. Following headless chickens is another, but less useful, method to find one's keys.

The trick is to orchestrate precipitating events on purpose. This can be done by using the techniques and tools presented in the *Good Thinking Series* of books and hundreds of other sources in libraries, the Internet, etc.

There are innately highly-creative people. But even those without these exceptional gifts can learn to be more creative than they currently are, and to do it on purpose. A modern understanding of creativity recognizes that there are techniques available to assist anyone who wants to improve their creativity.

Thinking of process improvement and creativity as a learnable skills will encourage you to deliberately structure "precipitating events" that will more easily lead to "cognitive snaps" and "transformations," and fill your junk drawer with the ideas you're searching for in all areas of work—improvement, new products, new services, etc.

Precipitating Events – Why Do They Work?

You might consider that there are three types of

thinking:

- **Instinctive:** you decide "automatically"—you pin prick your finger and your hand moves away. Your ride your bike without a paper list of to do's.
- **Emotional:** you decide based on how it feels at the moment. "Oh one more beer is not going to hurt." This type of thinking uses the amygdala of your brain. It seems that when we as people get under stress, for some, anytime they're awake, we default to this level of thinking too often leaving us with decisions we later regret.
- **Intelligent:** you decide based on a comparison of your current options against your goals. This type of thinking engages the prefrontal cortex of your brain where the "executive functioning" takes place. This is where logical thinking occurs. This is the home of the decisions we're glad we made.

Precipitating events work because the engage the prefrontal cortex.

Inside the Box - The Brain's Workings - A Fundamental Primer

My work often presents clients with thinking styles or algorithms (process improvement, creative thinking skills, strategic planning, etc.) in seminars and facilitated meetings which promote or provoke new ideas that clients find valuable. I am, of course, curious if and how these techniques actually work, how a mental exercise can actually develop ideas, on purpose.

I have now twice attended a very helpful conference that has helped me: Hope College's (Holland, MI) Brain and Learning Institute (*www.braininstitute.org*). One speaker, Dr. Marcia Tate (*www.developingmindsinc.com*) provided a very helpful, visual reference of the brain. Place your hands in a praying position. Your hands are about the size of your 3.5 pound brain which is most like a combination of JELL-O and tofu. Your folded hands represent the two halves of your brain. Your thumbs represent the left and right prefrontal cortexes where you do most of your logical thinking and decision making. Your brain includes about 100 billion neurons. Each neuron (cell body) surrounds a nucleus in its center, has a tail called an axon that sends information, and is surrounded by up to six thousand dendrites which receive information. Information is transferred from axons to dendrites via electrochemical impulses that jump the space from axon to dendrite called synapses. Learning grows dendrites—functional MRIs actually see the growth in the nodes on the dendrites as learning progresses.

Brain Friendly Learning

Innovation is fundamentally fast productive learning and implementing. Fast productive learning will happen best when it honors how the brain likes to learn.

What engages axons, and helps grow new dendrites, is great questions. Great questions act as great precipitating events. I call this phenomenon Yenta, after the matchmaker from Fiddler on the Roof. A great question is presented to the brain, the axons become engaged, new information is exchanged electro-chemically between the billions of axons and their dendrites, and Yenta shouts, "Have I got a match for you!" New ideas are formed (cognitive snaps) and new dendrites grow.

Great questions help us grow insights, dendrites, and knowledge. Great questions help us learn. When we ask and answer great questions deliberately, we choose to learn deliberately. The *Good Thinking Series: Collaborate* presents many tools—many questions—to promote and provoke learning. Deliberate learning helps us improve and innovate deliberately.

The *Good Thinking Series'* techniques and tools do not tell team members what to think, but *how*. Questions that are answered openly and honestly, with the help of data, in the company of the team members, generate dialogue and learning. This is the opposite of "group think."

Good Thinking Series, books 3 and 4 will help you learn how to deliberately structure "precipitating events" that will more easily lead to "cognitive snaps" and "transformations,"—the very ideas that you're searching for in all areas of work: improvement, new products, new services, etc.

3
Introduce Process Improvement Skills

Improvement and Innovation are Business Imperatives

We live in a competitive world. Commerce is now global and for us to succeed we must be able to compete with, and exceed, our competition in providing products and services to our global markets efficiently, effectively, and profitably.

To compete we must improve. To improve we must change. To change we must start doing something new, and stop doing what we have been doing that doesn't help anymore.

To compete we must innovate. To innovate we must be able to regularly develop new products, new services, and new attractions to customers to build market share and profitability.

Deciding to improve and innovate are decisions to learn, on an ongoing basis, throughout your organization, faster than your competitors.

Organization Improvement Options

Process improvement is one possible optional strategy

Imagine

an organization can choose to help improve its performance. Process improvement is one fundamental strategy to solve problems.

Another strategy to improve company performance is to work hard to develop leadership. Send people on multiple retreats to learn to get along with themselves and each other better. While this can improve one's personal confidence, without a way to think about and improve the "how" of how everything gets done in an organization, leadership development is necessary but insufficient. This could also include mergers and acquisitions and many others.

Woe be to the company or organization that thinks they're past all this. Process is how everything gets done every day—done well or done poorly.

The fundamental notion here is that every organization has waste in their processes — how they conduct their activities in every activity in their business— inside and outside their facility.

Some companies claim that they are OK, that they really don't need to work on improvement because they are profitable. This is like a boater saying he is OK because he can bail faster than the boat is leaking. Process improvement aims at plugging the leaks, starting with the big, easy ones.

Speed Bumps – News From the Front

Over the years I have been fortunate to present many keynote speeches, nationally and internationally. I enjoy seeing hundreds of new faces, eager to learn about Better Meetings, Planning Strategies, Leading Change, Collaboration Skills, and Creative Thinking Skills. I enjoy an hour of stimulating work, a fine meal, and an

30

applauding audience. What's not to like?

I get a chance in these presentations to ask questions and get a quick audience response. So while their reactions are not hard scientific data, I do notice some trends worthy of mention.

One question that I've been asking is, "How many of you work in organizations that can deliberately solve a problem, i.e. deliberately improve a process?" In other words, do they have improvement teams that use a structured improvement process (for example, PDCA, 8 D's, Kepner-Trego, etc.) to guide their thinking past the emotional and personality-based opinions to solid data-supported options? How many can identify possible root cause, conduct experiments to confirm the offending process steps, and successfully implement the improved process where applicable?

I should add that my audiences are primarily operational leaders from service and manufacturing companies, large and small, usually 50-90 in attendance: project managers, operation managers, HR leaders— people who have direct responsibility for leading the processes that determine a company's success.

To the question about a company-wide, or even group-local, improvement capability being in place and used, only about 10% of the audience raise their hands.

Another Perspective – News From the Whine Bar

I was once having lunch at a small restaurant at the Detroit airport. The spot was snug, and with all the tables very close to one another it was all too easy to hear what conversations were taking place all around you. To my left was a pair talking too loudly to ignore. It was a lengthy discussion of a particular meeting sequence that had occurred over the past few months, and by all accounts had not and was not going well. I heard phrases like, "Such a waste of time," and "Hardly anyone's prepared," and "Does Bob have any idea what we're thinking?" You can imagine the rest.

If this had been a manufacturing environment—say a cafeteria table off the manufacturing floor—the conversation might might have included, "Such a waste of time," and "No one knows what they're doing," and, "Wrong product in the wrong box," and, "Do we have any idea what the customer really wants?"

Throughout the *Good Thinking Series*, I'm encouraging you to think of a meeting, the most frequently-cycled business process in the world, as a decision-making factory. Continuous improvement ("CI") initiatives have taught us to look for and eliminate waste. No defects, and no whining.

So, back to the bistro in the Detroit airport. All these complaints were just running all over my lunch. Since I'm a pleasant, amiable sort of person, and consultant hearing a possible opportunity, I just had to say something. As they prepared to leave, I said, "Sounds like your meetings aren't going very well...? "You can say that again!" Chat, chat. I responded, "Has your organization implemented any continuous improvement teams?" "Oh, we're all over that stuff." And off they rushed. Not even a chance to exchange business cards—I just got an opportunity to improve my sales process.

I just sat there for a few minutes thinking about the phrase they left with, "Oh, we're all over that stuff." I detected a possible double meaning: 1) *We're done with the CI stuff—been there, done that;* or 2) *We're doing all sorts of CI stuff, all over like hair on a bear.* In either case, they were advertising their current reality.

So, in either case there seemed to be some active denial going on. In the first, if they were done with CI, their meetings, and all their processes should be smooth, profitable, and generate little/no angst. In the second, if they were active with their CI efforts, that their meetings stunk suggests they are focusing on some of the processes, but not on the mother lode—how they conduct their decision making, how they conduct their meetings.

Things are the way they are because they got that way. Whether it's defective product or defective meetings, the results are the consequence of poorly constructed and managed processes. In many companies' CI efforts, many are seeing some results, but many are seeing too little results for the effort. In many companies, leaders and employees, many are putting up with awful meetings—sort of like how companies used to put up with bad products on the loading docks.

Please lead your organization to raise the bar. Don't put up with this stuff. You have the capacity to improve all your processes, meetings included. Just as you have learned not to put up with bad products or services, don't put with bad meetings. Use what you know about process improvement on meetings and enjoy the many benefits. See *Collaboration,* chapter 7, "Building a Collaborative Culture – One Big Step."

But We're So Busy

Given the casual examples provided above, apparently few companies actually either try to improve their processes, or realize the benefits of process improvement. We all know, and may work at, companies that are champion fire fighters. Every day is busy, busy, busy.

Fire fighting is addictive. The busyness and activity surrounding fire fighting looks so much like work that many are led astray by a wide variety of new topic-of-the-month initiatives. "Hey, what are you guys working on? Initiative A, B, C or D?" "Well, all of them, actually. Isn't that what we're supposed to do?"

Only after the actual results of fire fighting are honestly evaluated does enough frustration occur to move company leaders to take the time and resources to build an internal company wide change capability. Improve and innovate, deliberately. That will keep you plenty busy and productive.

Size of the Potential Waste

One set of numbers that floats around the consulting industry suggests that if an organization cannot or does not deliberately improve and innovate their organization, they are unknowingly spending 10-30% of their revenues generating waste.

Wow, that's a lot of waste.

Let's translate this into work hours. With eight hours in the work day and fifty-two weeks in the year, each employee represents 2,080 hours a year. With even 10% waste, each employee may be spending about 200 hours a year not adding value; just going about their business, responding to requests, you know, day-to-day stuff. Divided by forty hours a week, that's five weeks. Sort of like an extra, very long, paid vacation.

Considering the revenue and profit percentage points improving and innovating quickly adds to the bottom line, it's a wonder how some organizations can afford to spend so much time and resources on fire fighting.

Why Bother? Considerations About Process Improvement

A business argument (from Joseph Juran, an early quality guru) for this work describes a company whose goal is to generate more profit dollars, more extra money at the end of the year. Let's imagine they're a $50 million revenue company earning 5% profit, or $2.5 million per year. They want to double their profit dollars.

One strategy would be to increase capital and head count to increase the size and capacity of the organization to reach this goal. If the current system capability generates x and they want 2x, then they need twice the revenue, i.e. $100 million in revenues. But they would have to subtract the cost to double the organization's capability, so in fact they would need even more revenues, an even larger organization.

Another strategy would be to target the 10-30% of an organization's revenue being spent on generating waste. This waste is often hiding in their company processes. Here they would maintain the size of the organization but deliberately improve its capability. To earn an additional $2.5 million dollars, they would have to improve their processes only 5.3% ($2.5M new profit/$47.5M operating costs). Improving their processes only 10% would earn $4.7M extra profit dollars, without extra head count or additional capital in many cases; equipment is improved and not necessarily purchased.

This improvement can only occur when leaders and employees learn to think and act differently about waste. They should ask themselves the following questions, in sequence:

1. What does it look like?

2. Where is it hiding?
3. How can we reduce it?
4. How can we maintain the new processes?

The joke goes, "When fish get together to talk about their problems, they never talk about the water." Process improvement training teaches companies to talk about and improve the water.

And while it may be harder than closing the windows on a cold winter's day to reduce heat loss, companies can learn to think in ways supported by the improvement and innovation strategies and work deliberately to move this 10-30% out of the dumpster and onto their bottom line.

Toyota is one example of an organization that has embraced this approach very successfully.

"Brilliant process management is our strategy. We get brilliant results from average people managing brilliant processes. We observe that our competitors often get average (or worse) results from brilliant people managing broken processes."

—Mr. Cho, Chairman of Toyota

In my experience, process improvement—along with its associated tools and techniques—is one of the best ways to improve an organization's performance on a company wide scale.

Problem Solving and Process Flow Charts

Process Improvement is a business strategy to improve business performance. One of its fundamental uses is to solve problems. Solving problems, like most business tasks, involves making great decisions. In process improvement, flowcharts are the working document to guide your thinking during your pursuit of the causes of the problems. Just as you might use a map looking for treasure, or blue prints to show how a house under construction will look.

A flow chart can be a visually documented sequence of steps, each titled with a noun and a verb, that describes either how a process is currently operating, or how a process might operated in an improved state.

Simple Process Flow Chart
Macro Level Showing A Company
And Its Major Partners

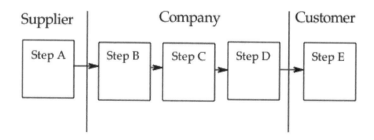

Process flowcharts help teams discuss and document the cause and effect relationships in their organizations.

Considerations About Chronic Process Problems

Improvement teams assigned to solve a problem are often working to change a chronic problem. If the problem had been easy, a fix might have been found without this extended level of effort or collaboration tool support.

An introduction to this section's header might read "Things have never been more as they are than right now." Chronic problems can be thought of as a natural result of their supporting process(es). Chronic problems are indications of current process capability. The problem, perceived as a gap between what one wants and what one has, is only the end point in a series of process steps. If we like the problem, too much of a good thing, we might just leave the process alone. If we do not like the problem, this book will offer suggestions of how to look at the problem and its supporting process(es) and how to modify the process(es) so that you can predictably end up with what you prefer.

Chronic problems cannot be addressed with quick fixes. A chronic problem requires a deeper search past lots of historical assumptions, misperceptions, and unhelpful opinions. Choosing to use a rigorous problem solving methodology should be accompanied by a discipline and patience to actually use the methodology to help you really find the root cause. Firefighting and quick fixes are evidence this discipline and patience is lacking.

Fundamentally, effective problem solving will have you more efficiently identify and modify the causes of a process to generate the results you prefer. It's like pursuing and finding a better cookie recipe, which is really a better sequence of steps that results in better cookies.

As a dialogue tool, like those presented in *Collaborate*, Process Improvement ("PI"), done well, follows a best practice sequence of good steps and tools, all of which help teams learn how to solve their problems by helping them learn what to do by asking and answering great questions. Process Improvement needs a great sequence of great questions to learn what is happening with a troublesome process..

Simple Improvement Process: Macro level showing the four improvement process steps

Solving problems is nothing new. It has occurred since the dawn of man. What has improved is the quality and sequence of the best practice questions, the tools and techniques.

Any modern version of a problem solving process includes the sequence of categories of questions: *Plan, Do, Check, Act.*

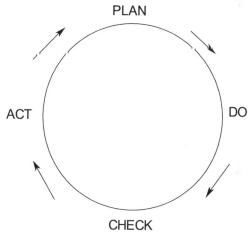

PLAN

ACT

DO

CHECK

Fundamental Improvement Process Steps

1. **Plan:** complete your team's preparation work.
2. **Do:** conduct experiment on your best guess for improvement.
3. **Check:** compare experiment results to your target improvement.
4. **Act:** implement improvement and create next plan, or revise plan and start again.

Like any good collaboration tool it helps teams collect and use data to learn, minimizing mere opinions or political agendas. In many cases, the four steps take the following portions of time: Plan 60%, Do 20%, Check 5%, Act 15%. Effective teams take the vast majority of their time preparing themselves to make good decisions to identify the most likely cause, craft an improved process to eliminate the problem, and prepare to conduct the experiment.

While there are many versions of PDCA improvement processes (8D's, Kepner, Tregoe, etc.), I strongly recommend that each organization learn to build and use their own. It may be attractive to copy another organization's improvement process, such as Toyota's. Successfully solving problems in an organization depends on that organization's skill set and culture. The next chapter will provide an overview of an example improvement process. At some point you will want to choose the titles of the major steps (mine has ten) and then the specific tools you will include to guide your teams while completing these steps.

There are probably a hundred tools that you could choose from to support your improvement process steps. To make your improvement process useful and effective, have your organization's team learn how to use a variety of tools on real issues and then choose which to include in your process.

Some helpful analogies: Learning to use and select tools is like tasting a number of dishes in a buffet line. Try many of them out but choose only enough that you'll really use, knowing you can go back, after you've mastered the first round, to select more to continue to build your improvement process. Learning to use and select tools is also like preparing young courtroom lawyers how to choose and present questions to a jury. You can't know it all in the first trial. As you grow to be a better lawyer, better questions will make your job easier.

Improvement Process – Leadership & Guidance Team Challenges

Upon learning about burned toast in an badly-run breakfast diner, the manager yells loudly in the kitchen at the cooks, "Darn it, you all better start making better toast, or else!" In a well-run restaurant, when a customer complains about burned toast, the manager works with the kitchen staff to learn about the variables that contribute to customer dissatisfaction, and helps the employees build a better toast-making process.

Another book could be written on how to prepare an organization to use improvement processes. Fundamentally, it would be a book to help leaders lead collaboratively. Many books have been written about the Toyota Production System, a comprehensive leadership model that uses process improvement as one of its tools. This approach is commonly called "Lean," as in lean manufacturing, lean service, lean office, etc. Hundreds, maybe thousands, of companies around the world have tried to successfully implement (copy) this approach. Toyota makes this easy, even going so far as to train both suppliers and competitors about how to follow this regimen.

It is very interesting then, with all the focus by the upper management of so many companies and all the associated millions of dollars spent to learn this approach, that the following is an objective report of their success to date (2011). Lean expert David Meier, author of *The Toyota Way and Toyota Talent* with Jeffrey Likert, writes "Our primary concern is the relatively low success rate of other companies that are on the lean journey. Our surveys indicate only one in five managers working on Lean are satisfied with the results."

Having worked with hundreds of improvement teams over the past thirty years, you won't be surprised to hear me suggest that the poor record of successful Toyota System implementations is so because the team members are not trained to collaborate. They're taught how to follow an improvement method but not how to work productively with each other. In a hockey analogy, they're put onto the ice trained to skate, but not trained to pass, shoot, or check. Improvement team meetings are all too often "polite, very nice."

In addition, these weak-performing teams are also most often led by senior leaders who do not know how to collaborate. And worse, some do not want to collaborate. It's my impression that these leaders cannot pass the reins to the employees. They want the power, they want the hierarchy, they want the status. And they want this more than the financial success available to more effective-thinking leaders. These leaders do not trust that the employees will do the work in the way that the leaders think they've asked for it to be done. There are many stories about companies, and even Toyota competitors, visiting the Toyota Manufacturing plant in Georgetown, Tennessee (where the Camry is built) and asking aloud how Toyota could take American workers and thinkers, and teach them to work together in ways that generate amazing results. Unless American leaders learn to think and behave collaboratively, all the time, they actually prevent the success available from the Toyota System.

Steps To Establish An Organization-Wide Improvement Capability

I recommend building your Company-Wide Improvement Capability (CWIC) in two stages. An outline of these stages is on page 59. Why Stage One and then Stage Two? Deltapoint, a Bellevue, Washington-based research organization which tracks data on organizations initiating continuous improvement, reports that seven of ten companies getting started have "false starts," and these organizations either stop or start over.

I believe organizations can succeed in being part of the three out of ten that succeed, but only by taking the time to build their own improvement capability, and by learning what does and does not work through practicing with a limited number of pilot projects before going company-wide.

Stage 1: Pilots
(L&GT: leadership and guidance team; IT: improvement team; ITL: improvement team leader; IPC: improvement process coach)

1. Leadership chooses to improve.
2. Leadership identifies guidance team.
3. Educate leadership and guidance Team (L&GT), and improvement process coach (IPC).
4. L&GT sets corporate vision and goals.
5. L&GT characterizes current situation and needs.
6. L&GT outlines first draft of CWIC Implementation Plan.
7. L&GT builds improvement process and support processes.
8. L&GT chooses pilot projects, improvement teams (IT).
9. L&GT and educate pilot project members.
10. ITs start pilot projects.

11. L&GT monitor and support pilot project members.
12. L&GT review results with team leaders, IPC, and IT and write draft rev 2 of CWIC implementation plan, improvement process, and support processes.

Stage 2 - Proliferation

13. L&GT chooses to proliferate improvement capability company-wide.
14. L&GT identify next target processes, identify team leaders.
15. IPC educates employees company-wide.
16. Team leaders implement improvement and departmental teams.
17. L&GT monitors and supports improvement and departmental teams.
18. L&GT review and revise CWIC Implementation Plan.

Improvement Process: Leadership & Guidance Team Pre-Work Summary

I prefer to identify four roles for improvement teams and their supporting leadership team:

- Leadership & guidance team
- Improvement team leader
- Improvement team members
- Improvement process coach

An organization's LGT includes the first and second level of leaders. This can often include a company president and their direct reports. I encourage this team to think about their IT's as spectacular investment opportunities. Considering a team can reduce the expenses in a targeted process by 10-30%, often with little or no capital, the improvement teams succeeding can be thought of as one of the primary money makers in an organization. It warrants and deserves their full attention and support.

I prefer that the LGT (leadership & guidance team) author and practice the improvement team's improvement process, the "Plan, Do, Check, Act" process, previously described. The LGT needs to know how to monitor, encourage, and fund their work, and how to pick and staff great improvement teams. The leadership & guidance teams must know what they are asking their improvement teams to do.

In selecting the first improvement teams, I ask that the LGT select at least four pilot teams during the organization's first use of its improvement process. This way if one of the teams does not reach their goals, the other three can represent what this new way of working can do for the organization. A single pilot team failing can set back an improvement capability by months.

Each pilot team should be assigned a problem, the result of a process, whose improvement would be significant. Don't assign them to solve something as hard as world hunger, and don't assign them something as inconsequential as improving the arrangement of the cafeteria tables. Ideally, each pilot team will complete work that encourages them to want to continue with this work, and impressive to the many employees and leaders on the side lines. The best case would be if you have a real need, a chronic problem that needs fixing, and a team that really wants to fix the problem. You are not only improving four processes, you are introducing the whole organization to a different way to think and work.

I recommend that the L&GT assign four pilot projects that are cross functional, meaning that they address processes that cross functional boundaries and that require working across functional silos. The following diagram shows an assigned process, steps A – E. The matrix below shows both the LGT, and who gets selected from each functional area to be part of this assigned process's improvement team: the person from that function who knows the process best. And yes, they're always the busy ones, because they're the heavy lifters. Do not assign people who aren't busy and need something to do. It's a death wish.

Preferably, people on these teams are good dealing with conflict, can work together productively, and just need better questions to guide their learning to discover the problem's cause. A team which would later be assigned a functional process is represented in the far right column.

Common Errors in Selecting Projects:

- Selecting a process that no one really cares about.
- Selecting a desired solution, instead of a process.
- Selecting a process in transition.
- Selecting a system to study, not a process.

Selection Considerations: Improvement Team

Assigned Process:

Organization/ Roles vs. Assigned Process:

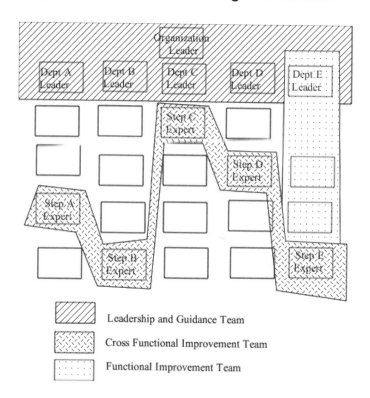

Improvement Team Member Training

Team Leader Training

The pilot project team leaders are responsible for leading their improvement team to achieving the process improvement targets assigned by the L&GT. Effective team leaders should have the following characteristics:

- Diverse skills and resources.
- A stake in the process.
- Authority to make changes.
- Clout and courage.

Their training should precede the beginning of the improvement team work and prepare them to:

- Anticipate and prepare for "speed bumps." These speed bumps can include social, political, budgetary—anything that could slow things down.
- Plan ahead a month. This allows the team leader to bring confidence and momentum into each improvement team meeting.
- Keep their eye on successful implementation. Like any good coach, help your team appreciate that their work is not done until the team receiving the improved processes is ready to, and wants to, take it over and make it work.
- Communicate frequently with L&GT. Coach the L&GT so they can provide "buy offs" and help at any time. Help the L&GT support the improvement team so the team feels in the loop but not micromanaged.
- Make full use of improvement process coach.
- Meet regularly with other Team Leaders; improvement process coach facilitates. One option is to hold monthly Team Leader Lunches. As-

semble over lunch in a quiet room and discuss highlights and low lights with other team leaders. This is a great way to help improvement team leaders appreciate that the troubles they are seeing with their teams and L&GT are likely the same. Discussing how to handle these normal developmental problems is very helpful to not only assist the team leaders but also build wider confidence and momentum in the pilot teams as a group.

- Team-meeting process. The team leader needs to be a task master about assigning all team members to lead improvement team meetings in some sort of regular schedule, and to really use the meeting process developed by the improvement team in improvement process step 1.

Team Training

I mentioned the characteristics of improvement team Members a few pages back while discussing the L&GT roles and duties. I like to have 4-6 improvement team members in addition to one improvement team leader on each team.

I prefer to train the pilot improvement teams with their team leaders and improvement process coach in a series of two-day seminars. This allows the whole teams to hear what the other teams will be working on while they learn how to use the improvement process steps and tools.

This training should be hands on having the team begin to use the improvement process from the beginning and include:

- Organization data. How does this assigned project fit into other organization plans and goals.
- Introduction (fundamentals, goals, decision making, people roles, definitions, implementation model). This is a run through of who will do what when how and why.
- improvement process (strategies, tactics, and tools). This helps the team appreciate the role and support the improvement process and its tools provide the team.
- Plan and Prepare (meetings process, plan and schedule). This asks the teams to develop and follow planning tools.
- Implementation Issues (leader fallibility, team dynamics). Here the teams discuss real speed bumps that may slow the team's progress.

Improvement Process Coach

Organizations should find an internal person who has extra training in project management, group process, and improvement process skills who can:

- Focus the team's process.
- Assist the improvement team leader in breaking down tasks.
- Work with team leader between meetings to plan upcoming meetings.
- Prepare and presents training.
- Help teams prepare presentations.

The improvement team leader is the improvement process coach's primary customer.

The improvement process coach is a proactive trainer and the process facilitator, helping the improvement team learn improvement process steps and tools as they need them, and keeping the pilot improvement teams on track, on schedule, and helping them to succeed. This includes coaching the team leader to monitor the L&GT so they are ready to support the improvement team at all times.

In many cases, organizations will find an external person to coach the pilot teams during the pilot phase. However, I strongly recommend that an internal person is assigned this role from the beginning and shadows the external person during the pilot phase. The internal improvement process coach will lead the proliferation of the improvement capability after the pilot phase.

Improvement Team Roles and Meetings

Assigned improvement teams ought to meet at least every other week for 60-90 minutes. Improvement teams need about twelve meetings to complete their work. Regular attenders should include:

- Improvement team leader: the person responsible for implementation of group's decisions, person given the role to be responsible for a great meeting.
- Improvement team members: functional or cross-function process step representatives.

Improvement team members should be assigned the following roles on a regularly rotating basis:

- Meeting leader: Uses improvement process steps and tools, and Meeting Process to guide the improvement team during each meeting.
- Improvement team recorder: captures and documents the meeting; keeps meeting minutes.

Occasional Attenders May Include:

- improvement process coach: aims to make group's work easier, keeps meeting on task, teaches team to use appropriate tools, manages participation, checks decisions, closes discussions, helps group keep track of time.
- Subject experts: internal and external, content providers.
- Customers and suppliers: internal and external, content providers.
- L&GT representative: interact most frequently with Improvement team leader and frequently reviews teams Storyboard. This person can make occasional cameo appearances at the meetings lending support but not advice. Make an impression, bring donuts.

Process Improvement Skills - Business Goals: Company-wide Improvement Capability

What can this look like when completed, after the pilot team period?

Your organization's L&GT identifies and prioritizes process-problems, and then assigns these as projects to improvement teams.

These teams then follow the organization's improvement process which guides them to talk with the process's customers, identify the problems, build a better process, confirm it works in a trial, and implement the improved process so it sticks.

You deliberately improve your organization one process as a time.

Helping a company learn to use process improvement effectively is most often a major cultural change, hence a significant change initiative. The purpose of pilot improvement teams is to help the organization learn what works best for them before they attempt to go companywide.

4
Practice Process Improvement Skills

This is an overview of the improvement process described on page 59. Later in this chapter we will examine the steps in greater detail. First, let's review the major steps that I find most useful in condensed format.

Improvement Process Steps Example (Mini View):

PLAN

1. Establish Team
2. Define Problem, Schedule Work
3. Describe Current Situation, Gather Data
4. Analyze, Prioritize Causes
5. Modify Flow Chart

DO

6. Try Out Improvements

CHECK

7. Study Results

ACT

8. Standardize Improvements

PLAN

9. Plan Next Improvements
10. Celebrate

The following more detailed improvement process I will use as an example includes the tools I find most useful. These steps and tools represent a fairly comprehensive collection of questions chosen and sequenced to assist a team working to solve a chronic problem. It is unlikely you would use each tool under each step. I would recommend though that you complete each and every step, in this sequence, coming to learn and use the tool that best helps you complete each step.

Like any search activity, this process with its steps and tools does not come with a guarantee that you will find your problem's root cause in a single pass with this process. I am confident though that if you are disciplined and deliberate to complete all the steps and the tools you choose, you are far more likely to find your cause in less time, and end with a team that understands why they chose to change their process a certain way, and what they need to do to make the change a true success.

While I will present the steps and tools in the sequence you would likely use them, consider sharing the work of learning the different tools. By lottery, assign a few tools to each member for the next few steps or so. I call the learners tool champs. Then when it's time to use a particular step and tool someone on the team can step forward and show the team how to complete the exercise.

Don't expect perfection. Do expect improvement.

Improvement Process Steps and Tools, Example (Mini-View with Applicable Tools):

1. PLAN - ESTABLISH TEAM

- Assigned Team Goals (page 59)
- Great Team Traits (page 60)
- Collaboration Skills (page 61)
- Meeting Process (page 62)
- Improvement Process (page 65)
- Storyboards (page 65)
- Work Room Set Up (page 66)

2. PLAN - DEFINE PROBLEM, SCHEDULE WORK

- Charter (page 68)
- SMARTR Criteria (page 70)
- Scoreboard (page 71)
- Systematic Diagram (page 72)
- Gantt Chart (page 73)
- Storyboards (page 75)

3. PLAN - DESCRIBE CURRENT SITUATION, GATHER DATA

- Big Picture (page 76)
- Process Flow Chart (page 78)
- Customer Research (page 80)
- P/R Measurements (page 82)
- Company Records (page 83)
- Relationship Diagram (page 84)
- Value Chain (page 86)
- Cross-Functional Process Map (page 87)
- Work Flow Diagram (page 88)
- Kano Model (page 89)
- Moments of Truth (page 91)
- Check Sheet (page 93)
- Run Chart (page 93)

4. PLAN - ANALYZE, PRIORITIZE CAUSES

- Scoreboard (page 93)
- Histograms and Run Charts (page 94)
- Cause and Effect Diagram (page 94)
- Flowchart Bingo (page 96)
- Force Field Diagram (page 98)
- Pareto Diagram (page 99)
- Impact EASE Diagram (page 101)
- Waste Search (page 102)
- Interrelationship Digraph (page 103)
- Prioritizing Process (page 105)
- Scoreboard (page 105)
- Brainstorming (page 105)
- Multivoting (page 105)
- Decision Matrix (page 106)

5. PLAN - MODIFY FLOW CHART

- Process Flow Chart with P/R Measurements (page 106)
- Benchmark (page 108)
- Leadership Buy Off #1 of 2 (page 110)

6. DO - TRY OUT IMPROVEMENTS

- Process Flow Chart with P/R Measurements (page 111)
- Check Sheet (page 111)
- Run Chart (page 111)
- Process Decision Program Chart (page 111)

7. CHECK - STUDY RESULTS

- Check Sheet (page 113)
- Run Chart (page 113)
- Histogram (page 113)
- Charter (page 113)

- Scoreboard (page 113)
- Show Me the Money (page 113)
- Leadership Buy Off #2 of 2 (page 113)

8. ACT - STANDARDIZE IMPROVEMENTS

- Collaboration Skills (page 114)
- Customer Research (page 114)
- Systematic Diagram (page 114)
- Process Decision Program Chart (page 114)
- Gantt Chart (page 114)

9. PLAN - PLAN NEXT IMPROVEMENTS

- Purpose, Vision, Goals, etc. (page 114)
- Leading Change (page 114)
- Customer Research (page 114)
- Scoreboard (page 114)
- Establish Team (page 114)

Improvement Process Steps Example (Micro View with Instructions):

Step 1. PLAN: ESTABLISH TEAM

The purpose of the first step is to help an improvement team get off on the right foot. Appreciate that, likely, this group of people have not worked together before, on this problem/assigned process, or with the discipline provided by the improvement process. In this step the team will build shared understanding of what they are being asked to do, and how they will work together.

ASSIGNED PROCESS, GOALS

This first step represents the topic of the pilot team's

work for the next few weeks and months. Team members may not at this point know how to think of their assignment as an endpoint in a flowchart. The team leader will develop these skills as the need occurs. An example of an introduction to a just assembled team meeting for the first time: We have been assigned a project which will ask us to reduce the throughput time on a particular process, manufacturing or service, from a current measured level to a improved measured level.

GREAT TEAM TRAITS

Great Team Traits provides a team an opportunity to consider, list, discuss, and prioritize the behaviors a team would prefer to see during its project work.

Process. At your team table:

1. Individually and silently brainstorm with Post-Its what your successful team is going to be like. What are the characteristics of successful team contributors? What will success look like at the major milestones? Describe the journey and the arrival.

2. Have the team meet at a flip chart and present and discuss each person's ideas, one person at a time presenting one idea at a time. Continue placing and discussing until all the ideas are posted.

3. As a team, create an affinity diagram on a flip chart by sorting the team's Post-Its into "natural catego-ries". For example: Accountable, Timely, Hard Worker, Good Listener, etc.

4. Write category headings at the top of each group.

5. Discuss insights about the resulting chart. "Does this chart represent what we as a team want to do?"

You have created a "Great Team Traits" scoreboard for your own team. Use it as a reference point when monitoring and evaluating your team's performance. For example when it's time to assess a team's progress, direct the team's attention to the Great Team Traits flip chart and ask the team "How are we doing? Suggestions for improvement?"

Teams can also raise the bar. If they think there is an area for improvement, they can add new success criteria they want to honor. This exercise is also a great icebreaker for new teams with the advantage that you are creating a useful tool and not just talking about your favorite color or what day of the week you'd like to be. A flip chart of this criteria should be posted in the workroom during each team meeting.

COLLABORATION SKILLS

The team leader introduces the definition that productive collaboration works to complete two tasks: build effective decisions while building effective support. This should include a quick discussion of the behavior options stressing that the team's goal will be to work in the collaboration corner as much as possible.

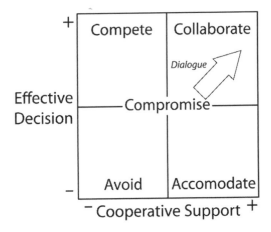

The improvement team will have better results in less time with less work when each member actively contributes to all the team's tasks working hard to build decisions they support.

MEETING PROCESS

This exercise will provide a process for the improvement team to use each meeting. It is the team's micro-process for getting work done. The improvement process (PDCA with tools) is the improvement team's mini-process.

Process. With your improvement team:

1. **Document and discuss current reality about how meetings go in your organization.**

    Using Post-Its, silently brainstorm the characteristics of meetings that you currently do not like. Think about awful meetings you've been part of. What do you not want to see in any of your improvement team meetings?

Write "Meeting Problems" at the top of a flip chart. Meet as a group and place one Post-It up at a time, one person at a time, like playing a card game where each person presents an idea when it's their turn. There should be lots of talk about each idea, include war stories about how this characteristic negatively affects a team's performance.

When the Post-Its are all on the flip chart, then silently organize the Post-Its into groups where the ideas belong together, they are similar. For example this group of ideas is about having an agenda, this group is about getting things done, etc. Finally rank the groups of ideas by their impact on a team's performance. Which is the worst restraining force, the next, etc.? This step is just like the previous Great Team Traits exercise. This flip chart with the Post-Its organized by group is called an Affinity Diagram.

This flip chart now represents the customer complaints for this team's meetings. The next steps of this exercise should provide a meeting process and ground rules that eliminate these problems.

2. Document and discuss your team's pre-ferred meeting process.

Using Post-Its, silently brainstorm the positive characteristics of great meetings. Think about great meetings you've been part of. What do you want to see part of your meetings? What new steps can eliminate the problems listed in this exercise's first step?

Write "Meeting Process" at the top left of a flip chart, and "Meeting Ground Rules" at the top right of the flip chart.

Using the brainstormed ideas, build a process flow chart underneath the Meeting Process flip chart along the left side, top to bottom, with those Post-Its that show sequence.

List those ideas that do not show sequence (could occur anytime during the meeting) under the Meeting Ground rules heading. Do include any new ideas as they occur to you as you work through this exercise.

3. Review your Meeting Process and Ground rules.

Add to the bottom of the flip chart an area titled "Team Assessment Criteria" and list how you can build self control into your meetings. Examples might include:

- Are we (am I) following the meeting process?
- Are we (am I) following the ground rules?
- Are we achieving the goals of our meeting?

Do benchmark other team's processes, ground rules, and team assessment criteria. Do they have any ideas you'd like to include in yours?

Build and begin to use this process with a small group which meets regularly. When you are dissatisfied with your meetings over a period of time, modify. Do police yourselves during the meeting. Do not rely on the meeting leader to take care of this. If you see someone not using the meeting process or ground rules, call them on it. Care enough to use this tool to help you have great meetings.

See *Good Thinking Series,* book 2, *Collaborate,* chapter 7, "Building a Collaborative Culture: One Big Step," for a full treatment of this topic.

IMPROVEMENT PROCESS

Introduce the team to the steps and tools of the organization's improvement process. Emphasize that the purpose of this process and regimen is to guide the improvement team as it works on a chronic problem. It does not represent busy work. It is likely that teams will resist this seeming bureaucracy. Improvement teams that complete their work with the aid of the improvement process are most often strong advocates for the improvement process as the organization moves ahead proliferating the use of this approach. A flip chart of this process should be posted in the workroom during each team meeting.

STORYBOARDS

The Storyboard is a dynamic sequence of flip charts, at least one flip chart sheet for each improvement process step, that serves as a workplace for the improvement team. Use to document the improvement team's work as they progress through their improvement process. Best placed where both L&GT members and employees can easily see the charts in everyday movement around your company.

The columns below represent improvement process steps 1-6.

Establish Team	Define Problem	Describe Current Situation	Analyze, Prioritize Causes	Modify Flow Chart	Try Out Imprvmnts
•assigned process	•brainstorm	•process flow chart	•brainstorm	•process flow chart	•process flow chart
•meeting process	•affinity diagram	•rel diag	•cause/ effect dia	•P/R meas	•checksheet
•impmnt process	•scoreboard	•value chain	•pareto diagram	•buyoff #1 meeting notice	•run charts
•leadership buyoff criteria	•Gantt chart	•cross functional process map	•decision matrix	•etc	•etc
•etc	•etc	•etc	•etc		

One client placed their four pilot team storyboards in a hall way between the cafeteria and the work place. As a person would walk by, motion detectors would engage a series of lights that shown on the charts drawing lots of attention and interaction from the passers-by.

You can also inform the employees not on the pilot teams that they too can interact with the storyboards by placing special colored Post-Its on the charts asking questions or making suggestions. This works as a group-sized, whole company, chat room.

WORK ROOM SET UP

Arrange your workroom and your resources to allow you easy access to your meeting materials (markers, Post-Its, flip chart paper, etc.) and guiding tools: Great Team Traits, Meeting Process, improvement process, and Storyboard. Ideally you can set up your room and leave it. Otherwise you can decide how you want to make your room as portable as possible.

Your storyboard needs to be accessible to your L&GT.

If you cannot dedicate a place to put your charts, consider finding a long (twenty feet long, three feet wide) sheet of paper to serve as the back of this sequence of flip charts. You can unroll the part of the Storyboard you need to work on and use the rolled ends as a support on a table.

PLAN: ESTABLISH TEAM. Summary.

Done well, Step One will result in an improvement team clear on its purpose and processes and eager to proceed. This improvement process step and others can be completed during a two-day training session that would have all four pilot teams attending.

Step 2. PLAN: DEFINE PROBLEM, SCHEDULE WORK

The purpose of Step Two is to define, organize, and schedule the work of the improvement team to take place over the course of the assignment.

CHARTER

A charter lists expectations within a team and/or between an team and their sponsor. The format of the charter provides a sequence of very useful questions. A charter can help:

1. An improvement or innovation team sponsor (L&GT representative) to think through their request to improve the chances of the impact of the assignment, or
2. The team leader to negotiate accountability for the assignment, or
3. The L&GT representative and improvement team leader pair to have a reference for their shared assignment.

Each player works hard to support this completed document before and after work begins.

DOCUMENT FORMAT:

TEAM CHARTER - SPONSOR PORTION

- *Project Title:*
- *Project Team Leader Name:*
- *Objective:* The end goal for this specific team ("Where are we going?"). Objectives should be

quantifiable (e.g. reduce scrap, increase productivity) and should be expressed in metrics with actual numbers.

- *Why Is This Important:* Explain how the objective evidence supports the organization's business goals.
- *Team Members & Skills:* Combination of team members to support the project, the skills needed, and any additional resources needed.
- *Boundary Conditions:* Include expectations for the project—what you can and cannot do. Boundary conditions may include limitations (i.e. need more manpower, or more overtime).

TEAM CHARTER - TEAM PORTION

- *Deliverables:* Tangible evidence of work done in support of team objective. Deliverables should be decided upon by team and due dates shown on work plan.
- *Metrics:* Quantifiable measurement (trend chart) directly related to objective, showing level of success.
- *Current Condition:* Establish current condition at beginning of project specific to metric.
- *Target Condition:* Desired state of metric upon completion of project.
- Ground Rules. Ground Rules include information on how the team will work together, when and where to meet, how does the team handle disputes.
- *Estimated Completion Date:*
- *Considerations:* I prefer that Sponsor Portion is developed together with the project sponsor and the project team leader, and the Team Portion by the whole team

SMARTR CRITERIA

Another way to clarify the components of your improvement team's goals.

Use **SMARTR** criteria to write useful objectives:

S – Specific. Are we clear about what is to be done? Clearly states the expected outcome or result for which an employee will be held accountable. The outcome is linked to overall business objectives.

M – Measurable. How will we know if it has been achieved? States the criteria that will be used to measure performance and make sure that the objective has been accomplished.

A – Accountable. Do we have the capabilities to be successful? Falls within an employee's primary area of responsibilities. Is this assignment aligned with larger company goals?

R – Realistic. Reasonable chance of achievement.

T – Time bound. When does it have to be completed? States the specific time frame in which it is to be accomplished.

R – Resources. What will it take (money, headcount, etc) to complete this task?.

Example:

FROM Improve business

TO Team ABC will generate 15% increase in billings in *xyz* market segment by January 20*xx*; budget $25,000.

SCOREBOARD

The Scoreboard serves a reference point for "success as measured by..." Sometimes also called KPI (key process indicators). It can be thought of as your work's dashboard; as with a car, what sort of indicators would you prefer to have. Only have an odometer on a car would be foolish. Only measuring financial results would be foolish. Some of the scoreboard's metrics should address upstream process steps that support a successful result downstream.

Process:

Working as a team, brainstorm success characteristics with Post Its, post on a flip chart with lots of discussion, group the Post Its into similar topics, and title the groups. The titles are your Scoreboard components.

Example Criteria

Scoreboard: QCDISM; (success as measured by...)

Quality
• Complaints on fewer than 5% orders.
• Measurable improvement on 75% of our processes.

Cost
• Operating at or below operating expense plans.

Current Programs
• Supporting 15 programs as outlined in 2001 strategic plan.

New Programs
• Supporting two new programs per half-year as outlined in 2001 strategic plan.

Employee Morale
• Employee turnover less than 10% per year.

A "Balanced Scorecard" includes both leading and lagging measurables. Three of these indicators (learning and growth, internal business processes, and proactive customer support) monitor leading indicators, indicators of process steps up stream in the company's macro process that, accomplished, bode well for the fourth indicator (financial success) to occur predictably. As we all know, a stitch in time saves nine. When everybody completes the processes that support the employees, internal processes, and customers, we are likely to be financially successful.

SYSTEMATIC DIAGRAM

The Systematic Diagram, also called the Tree Diagram, or the Dendogram, is a brainstorming planning format. This tool uses a flip chart and Post-Its to help a team identify and arrange paths and tasks to achieve primary and supporting goals.

Process:

1. Complete brainstorming exercise listing all steps required to complete project.

2. Arrange the steps in the following manner:

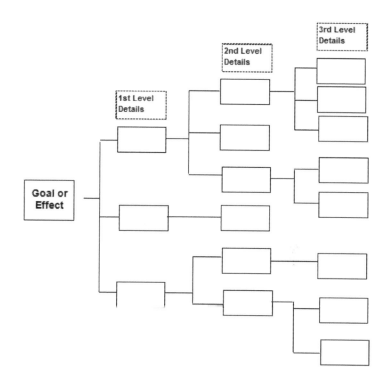

This is best done with the whole improvement team so everyone can contribute to the brainstorming and arrangement of the planning steps they will be responsible to complete. This tool is not the same as the improvement process. The Systematic Diagram is a planning tool to help the improvement team schedule the work necessary to complete the improvement process.

GANTT CHART

This tool was named after Henry Gantt (1861-1919), an American mechanical engineer and management consultant. Gantt charts were employed on major infrastructure projects including the Hoover Dam and Interstate Highway System.

Use the Gantt chart as a project management tool (for example instead of the Systematic Diagram) to clarify order and length of a project's assignments. The Gantt chart highlights sequence of assignments and shows when assignments can be serial or parallel.

Process

With the help of the whole improvement team:

1. List all the assignments and sub-assignments. This is easy and flexible with Post-Its.
2. Identify the required sequence of the assignments and place these steps in subsequent rows.
3. Identify which assignments must happen in series and which can happen in parallel. Two assignments in series shows that the first assignment must be completed before the second assignment can begin. For example, while looking at the Loan Process Schedule diagram, the team cannot begin to enter the data until they have completed receiving the request. This is shown by the project time lines in the two subsequent rows stop and start at the same time.

    Two assignments in parallel, at least to some degree, shows that a following step can be initiated before you complete the previous assignment. For example, on the next page the team can begin to review the loan before they complete entering the data. This is shown by the project time lines in the two subsequent rows overlap.

4. Present the assignments in the following manner:

EXAMPLE - LOAN PROCESS SCHEDULE

	Monday	Tuesday	Wednesday	Thursday	Friday
Receive Request	▬				
Enter Data		▬▬▬▬			
Review Loan			▬▬▬▬		
Inform Customer					▬▬

I prefer that the improvement teams uses the Gantt Chart as a dialogue tool, using the format to present, discuss, and place the assignments in the order the team supports, indicating the length of an assignment that the team agrees to, and collectively has the team ending the project assignment "on time."

Like other dialogue tools, it's a great place to discuss with data about how long things need to take, and which assignment ought to follow or precede another.

STORYBOARDS – Introduced in Step One

Use collaboration tools to build both good decisions and good support with each tool for each step in the improvement process. Do most/all of the work with the whole team attending and work with the data and flip charts up on the wall. The flip charts completed for each step should be included in sequence on the Storyboard.

Step 3. PLAN: DESCRIBE CURRENT SITUATION, GATHER DATA

In Step Three, the improvement team spends the time necessary to best understand the current reality of the assigned problem and process. In comparison with a doctor visit, this goes past the normal examination room chat. This includes data gathering procedures to really get to the underlying issues causing the problem.

It is important to document your troublesome process as it is, not as you'd like it to be.

It is important to challenge someone's perception of how a process is happening. In the best case scenario the listener will not take the challenge personally; they will say, "That's how I see it. Let me show you." And the improvement team heads out to where the process is occurring and sees for themselves what's really happening.

Appreciate that the assigned problem is chronic; no other team to date has figured out how to improve this process, how to eliminate this problem. It is not going to be easy. It will take new questions with new answers to help the team learn what it needs to know to solve the problem.

BIG PICTURE

This sequence of steps is a great way to build shared understanding of an improvement or innovation team's starting point. Big Picture is more of an approach and a collection of tools than one tool. The tool's name speaks to the breadth of view recommended for the improvement team at this point in the improvement process.

Process:

1. State the goal: **Improve the output of our candy-making process.**
2. Develop a scoreboard to measure success for your opportunity statement.
3. This step gives the sequence its name. On a flip chart or two document the situation as part of a system, as part of a big picture. As a team draw a detailed diagram of the problem and the area that surrounds it. Lots of details about the components and the relationships between the components.

In this step you want to emphasize the goal of this step is to document current reality, not the preferred state. There are a number of models in this chapter that can assist (details found elsewhere in this book and also in *Collaborate*). These will be described in detail in other improvement process steps. They are also included in *Good Thinking Series* Book 2 – *Collaborate: Tools and Techniques for Effective Meetings*. Some include:

- Relationship Diagram: show how the respective individuals/departments work in a matrix of relationships.
- Process Flow Chart: this document will show the sequence of the steps to complete.
- Value Chain shows columns of respective vertical processes allowing for appropriate connections between the processes.
- Workflow Diagram shows how people are moving around in the work area.

Discuss the ways in which each component of the problem affects the system and the situation's goals. This step's purpose is to feed a deep dialogue about the opportunity and anything and everything that might be related to the opportunity. One helpful addition is to use red colored markers to identify components on your drawing that are opposing your goals, and green for components that are supporting your goals.

PROCESS FLOW CHART

The process flow chart may well be the most useful tool to help improvement teams talk about how things happen, and how they should happen. Process flow charts are visual maps that show the cause and effect steps and sequence of how work gets done. Appreciate that the process flow chart format is another way to brainstorm ideas. The accuracy of the flow chart must be confirmed with data.

Process flow charts can be drawn at any level of detail. Here I am showing three levels: macro, mini, and micro.

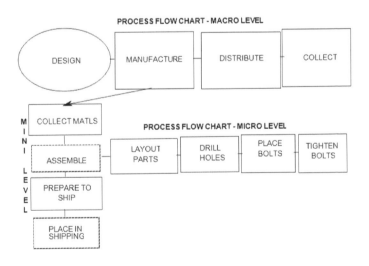

- Macro (big fundamental steps),
- Mini, (smaller fundamental steps), and
- Micro (a level of detail which allows you to document root causes).

When trying to solve problems, work first to identify how the work is actually being done by documenting the process where it's happening, with the people doing the work, and with data from the process.

If you're trying to solve a problem, appreciate that the flow chart you draw, if accurate, describes a process that creates the problem.

Process, Example:

1. Assemble the people who most often do the work, at their place of work. Be prepared to gather data out in the work place to document the process.
2. Identify the audience you are preparing the process flow chart for. How much detail do they need?
3. Choose the start point and end point of the process you want to focus on. Represent process steps in boxes and describe each step with nouns and verbs.
4. Fill in the steps between the start and end points.

Word has it that way back in 1989, when Xerox won its first Malcolm Baldrige quality prize, about 75% of their improvements came from just documenting their processes.

Imagine your team sitting in front of a few flip charts and documenting how everyone on a team actually completes a particular task. This open conversation will often uncover inconsistencies about how people are interpreting instructions and carrying out their activities.

5. Complete the chart and confirm for accuracy.

The conversation that develops this chart should be honest and robust. Using a flip chart and Post-Its allows flexibility for changes and improvements.

Flow charts would be used next in the improvement process to document the preferred sequence of new steps that would generate a better result.

Search for "process flow chart" on Google Images for lots of examples.

CUSTOMER RESEARCH

Successful business depends on the regular transfer of value from one company to another—from the provider to the customer. Knowing what your customer wants and will want is crucial to your success.

Establish and use a process to learn the "voice of the customer." This is one way to gather your customers' feedback. There are many sources and organizations who can help you dig deeper to help you learn what your customers would really like to see from your organization.

Serious customer research can include professional organizations able to solicit analyze statistically valid customer data.

Example Process:

1. Prepare yourself for a "people to people" process. Study your customers history, their interests, and their company culture.

2. Document the combined process that you and the customer share—your process and theirs (with a value

chain for example). Appreciate that your process is upstream from theirs, and that your customer uses the outputs of your process. On this flow chart clarify your process's inputs and outputs, and the customer's process's inputs (your outputs) and their outputs.

3. Prepare and list the questions you will ask the customer to gain insights into the combined process and what the customer likes and dislikes about both your produce and your service.

4. Choose the method you will use to collect data.

   Options include:
   • surveys: phone, face-to-face, internet survey tools
   • focus groups
   • on-line research
   • user groups
   • voice mail

Regardless of which method you use to collect a larger body of data, do visit a representative group of customers to confirm the data you collected.

5. Before you visit with the customer, practice your questions and interviewing process. It's best to discover what you like to do differently in a practice session with your own teammates, and not in front of the customer.

6. I recommend interviewers visit with the customer in pairs.

7. Meet with the customer at their facility. After introductions walk their process to see how your product/ service is actually used by the customer.

8. Ask your questions and record your data.

9. Confirm your understanding of what you learned during the visit with a review of your data with your customer host.

10. Send thank you note and provide them a copy of your visit results.

11. Use what you learned from a number of customers to improve the processes that support your products and services.

P/R MEASUREMENTS

Use this tool to document and clarify the locations and metrics of your process flowchart feedback loops. Feedback loops are questions within or at the end of a process flow chart that ask if certain conditions are met at that point in the process. If so, move on. If not, the feedback loop should direct the process owner to a corrective step. Your goal is to identify and implement measurements that allow you to monitor a process while it is operating and prevent process errors.

Here is an example of a flowchart that describes how a product moves from the supplier, through an organization, and to the customer.

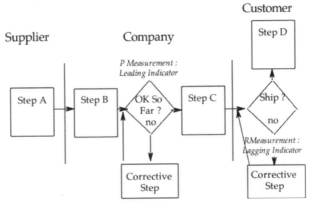

For simplicity I have shown only two feedback loops:

1. After Step B, is the product good so far? No defects? No problems?
2. After Step C, is the product good to ship? No defects? No problems?

In both cases, if the answer is no, the product moves to a corrective step before it can re-enter the process.

Our goal is to provide a defect-free product to the customer. I would prefer to identify any possible problems up stream in my process so I can either prevent the problems, or catch the product from moving on if it is defective. It is helpful to have both P and R measurements.

Feedback loops upstream to prevent problems (P - process, preventative, proactive, etc), and downstream (R - result) to confirm the product has no problems and is ready to ship.

An improvement team's goal is to place a sufficient number of P measurements in a process to prevent any possible defects, and assure preferred results at the R measurement. A second level of P measurements can help reduce waste.

COMPANY RECORDS

I will mention here what may be obvious: improvement teams should make good use of any current data available that would assist the team in learning more about the current reality of the assigned process. This can certainly include conversations with current or past process owners and anyone who may know about the process and how it got the way it is.

RELATIONSHIP DIAGRAM

A relationship diagram helps a team identify the components of an organization's system and the relationships between those components. The components are most often functional departments that play a role in the assigned process. This tool is often used when teams are beginning or reviewing their macro-level goals. Can be used in conjunction with a cross functional process map to highlight sequence.

Process:

1. Starting with a flip chart, place "function boxes" of company functions (sales, customer service, manufacturing, R&D, etc.) in center of a flip chart. Using Post-Its makes this flexible.

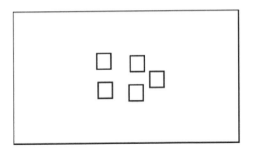

2. Draw a box around the functions that represent the organization.

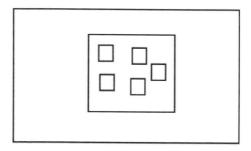

3. Place "function boxes" of company-partner functions (customers, suppliers, delivery, banks, shareholders, etc.) outside the box.

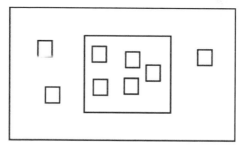

4. Draw single-ended arrows between function boxes and identify what value information, orders, money, ideas, capital, etc.) is transferred from whom to whom; write this on the arrow line.

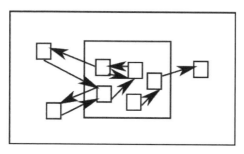

5. Discuss findings with team.

Like many other "current reality" brainstorming tools, the dialogue that helps build this diagram must be open and honest. When done, it's sort of like a circuit diagram. We might ask, "Where are the shorts?" Where should there be a relationship line and there isn't, or where does the line represent a troubled relationship?

VALUE CHAIN

Teams can use a value chain to brainstorm, confirm, and document, how value transfers between company and company-partner groups through a macro level process flow chart. The macro components of a company's system are represented in the chart below:

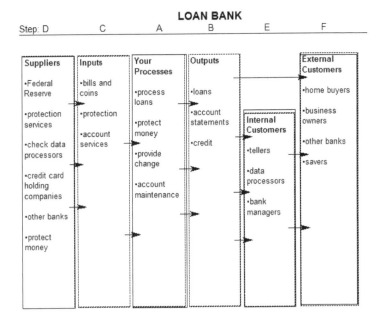

LOAN BANK

Step: D   C   A   B   E   F

Suppliers	Inputs	Your Processes	Outputs		External Customers
•Federal Reserve	•bills and coins	•process loans	•loans		•home buyers
•protection services	•protection	•protect money	•account statements	Internal Customers	•business owners
•check data processors	•account services	•provide change	•credit	•tellers	•other banks
•credit card holding companies		•account maintenance		•data processors	•savers
•other banks				•bank managers	
•protect money					

From left to right: suppliers, who provide my process's inputs, which my processes use to generate outputs (products and services) for both internal and external customers.

CROSS FUNCTIONAL PROCESS MAP

This tool's format clarifies cross functional responsibilities of a process flow chart. This tool can clarify how functions in an organization complete their work together. This tool shows relationships and sequence. The relationship diagram shows interdependencies.

Process:

1. Assemble the people who most often do the work, at their place of work. Be prepared to gather data in the work place to document the process.
2. Identify the audience you are preparing the process flow chart for. How much detail do they need; macro (big fundamental steps), mini, (smaller fundamental steps), and micro (a level of detail which allows you to document root causes).
3. Complete the macro level flow chart.
4. Identify which functions complete which steps. (bank manager, word processing, etc).
5. List functions on the y-axis of a matrix, with time-sequence along the x-axis.
6. Position process steps in the appropriate row and identify the sequence of steps with arrows.

Example, Loan Process:

This diagram shows both the macro level process flow chart above the dark horizontal line, and the cross functional process map below.

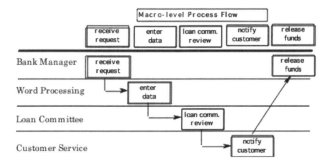

The first benefit comes from using this format to document current reality. How is the process really being conducted. Walk it through right in the workplace to confirm.

Then on another chart identify your preferred routing.

Doing this with either a white board or flip chart and Post-Its allows flexibility as you learn how things are, and how you'd like them to be.

WORK FLOW DIAGRAM

Use to clarify the pattern, distance, and frequency of movements of people, materials, documents, and information in processes. Most often developed as a bird's eye view. Should be developed to an accurate scale.

The impact of this tool comes from the "picture" of the process. Excessive distances and frequent trips are easy to see.

Process:

1. If possible, assemble your team at the actual site of process.
2. Walk through and document a "bird's eye view" sequence of steps in the process.

3. Complete another workflow diagram after you have improved the layout of the work area to confirm the desired improvements.

Bird's Eye View of Work Area:

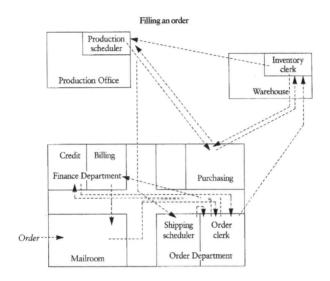

From *The Quality Toolbox*, by Nancy R. Tague (1995, ASQC Press; a great resource for problem-solving tools).

KANO MODEL

The Kano model can be used as a brainstorming format to help a team identify customer expectations, wants, and pleasant surprises.

The purpose of the tool is to differentiate product and service offerings. Done well it requires benchmarking and research to support the tool's brainstorming with data, not just opinions.

Process:

The original Kano Model will look like a graph with four quadrants with a diagonal line running from lower left to upper right. Time titles the horizontal coordinate, quality titles the vertical coordinate. This diagonal line emphasizes that the expectations of customers improve over time.

Below the diagonal line represents basic attributes. The diagonal line represents performance attributes. The area above the line represents excitement attributes.

- **Basic Attributes** are unspoken but expected. Exclusion of these attributes in the product has the potential to severely impact the success of the product in the marketplace. An example would be any new car buyer expects there to be a spare tire in the trunk. That it's there is no big deal. If it was found missing, especially on a desolate road with a flat tire in the rain, it becomes a very big deal.

- **Performance Attributes** are those for which more is generally better, and will improve customer satisfaction. Conversely, an absent or weak performance attribute reduces customer satisfaction. Of the needs that customers verbalize, most will fall into the category of performance attributes. An example would be the mileage the car can get. Many car buyers are selecting cars based on their mileage. ("Our car's mileage is as good or better than our competitors.")

- **Excitement Attributes** are unspoken and unexpected by customers but can result in high levels of customer satisfaction, however their absence does not lead to dissatisfaction. Excitement attributes often satisfy latent needs—real needs of which customers are currently unaware. In a competitive marketplace where manufacturers' products provide similar performance, providing excitement attributes that address "unknown needs" can provide a competitive advantage. Although they have followed the typical evolution to a performance and then became a threshold attribute, cup holders were initially excitement attributes. In New Orleans this is called a *lagniappe,* and means a little bit extra, like a "baker's dozen" (thirteen)—one extra, free!

You can also use a simple format. On a flip chart, draw lines to create three columns with the following titles: basic attributes, performance attributes, and excitement attributes. Then have the contributing team brainstorm, discuss, and place their data in the three columns, one column at a time. Lots of discussion, lots of data presentation. Lots of learning.

The overall goal of the exercise is to help the team confirm that they are quietly fulfilling the customers' basic attributes, advertising and attracting customers to the performance attributes, and finally, with both the basic and performance attributes fulfilled, then providing something to the customer that pleasantly surprises them, encouraging them to select your product or service.

MOMENTS OF TRUTH

Moments of Truth is a brainstorming format that can help a team identify customer expectations as the experiences your products and services. The purpose of the tool is provide a format to think about, document, and improve how an organization supports customers.

Process:

A helpful format for your work has the flowchart across the top horizontal of a flip chart. Once the process is settled, draw vertical lines so each process step has columns beneath. Then add three more open rows to receive your data. Titles for the rows: row 2 = voice of the customer; row 3 = current reality; row 4 = maintenance or correction plan.

1. Assemble the people who know most about your customers' interaction with your product and/or services.
2. Use a process flow chart as a format for your data collection and discussion. This is row 1.
3. Choose the start point and end point of the process you want to focus on.
4. List each process step as the customer would experience them. Represent process steps in boxes and describe with nouns and verbs. Post-Its are a good format for this work.
5. Include under each process step a prioritized list of what the customer wants at each step (row 2) , and the degree, positive or negative, that you are supporting the customer wants (row 3).

For the purpose of robust dialogue, to find the truth, people should challenge any possible inaccurate assumptions. Try, when possible, to back up the data in and under the process steps with data, not just opinions or hopes.

6. Finally, complete each column by identifying a maintenance or correction plan (row 4).

The notion of "moments of truth" comes from Richard Normann, who argues that a service company's overall performance is the sum of countless interactions between customers and employees that either help to retain a customer or send him to the competition.

The idea was later used by Jan Carlzon when he was CEO of Scandinavian Airlines back in 1986 and described the idea: "That spark and the emotionally driven behavior that creates it explain how great customer service companies earn trust and loyalty during "moments of truth:" those few interactions (for instance, a lost credit card, a canceled flight, a damaged piece of clothing, or investment advice) when customers invest a high amount of emotional energy in the outcome. Superb handling of these moments requires an instinctive frontline response that puts the customer's emotional needs ahead of the company's and the employee's agendas." (Adapted from Shep Hyken (hyken.com))

CHECK SHEET

Check sheets provide a simple format for data collection.

RUN CHART

Data from check sheets is often presented in a run chart which compares values to time, run charts are most useful to show data changes and trends.

Step 4. PLAN: ANALYZE, PRIORITIZE CAUSES

In Step Four, the improvement team digs deep to research, narrow, and select the possible root causes of the assigned problem. This step's tools should make it easier for improvement team members to see the multiple possible causes and to prioritize which causes addressed with have the most impact.

SCOREBOARD

The Scoreboard was presented earlier and is mentioned here to emphasize that any work in this step should be focused on accomplishing the criteria listed on the scoreboard.

HISTOGRAMS AND RUN CHARTS

Histograms and run charts are examples of data formats that make it easier for a team to see what a process has been doing. Histograms are bar graphs with time increments across the horizontal. Run charts are similar but connect the top data points to show trends.

CAUSE AND EFFECT DIAGRAM

The Cause and Effect Diagram is also called a "fish bone" for its appearance, and an Ishikawa Diagram for its originator. This tool is primarily a brainstorming format to assist a team in documenting possible root causes.

Process:

Volunteer to be the scribe who will enter team member ideas onto a flip chart sheet in the format listed below which everyone can see.

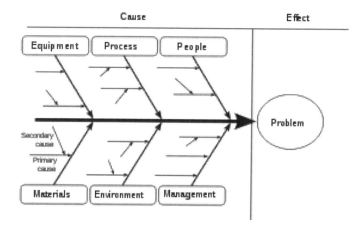

This is a free-flowing, open exercise where team members share their ideas. The fish bone titles (equipment, process, etc.) are included on the chart before the brainstorming to focus the team on the most common sources of problem's causes. You can also use your own.

Starting with one topic (bone)—equipment, for example—what are possible equipment-related causes to our current problem? As this first-level cause is written on one of the lines directly off the bone, you can then ask, "What contributes to this cause?" and write this idea off the first-level line as a second-level cause. One version of this sequence is called the "Five Why's." Ask why five times as you move through the sequence from a first-level cause all the way to a fifth-level cause.

Example Problem: Plane Late to Depart

Brainstorming on the "people" bone with the "five why's:"

- **Level 1:** Why is the plane late to depart? Maintenance need.
- **Level 2:** Why is there a maintenance need? Light went off on the cockpit dashboard.
- **Level 3:** Why did the light go off on the cockpit dashboard? Dashboard switch not operating correctly.
- **Level 4:** Why is the dashboard switch not operating correctly? Pilots often put their data binders on the dashboard while they're preparing for a flight breaking the switch levers.
- **Level 5:** Why do pilots often put their data binders on the dashboard while they're preparing for a flight? Binders are too large and heavy, and there is little space to place elsewhere.

This team would be encouraged then to move the pilot data to another provided surface or a small electronic device to eliminate the switch damage.

The purpose of the tool is to sequence great questions that answered with data by the team help the team to discover what is, and what is not, contributing to a problem.

Just because an item gets listed on the diagram does not mean it is actually a contributing cause. Resulting causes should be prioritized by likely impact and possibility, and pursued with further investigation.

FLOWCHART BINGO

The purpose of this exercise is to assist an individual or a team to wonder aloud about why a particular process is not performing as well as it might.

1. Document a currently troublesome process

Working alone or with a team:

a. Choose a troublesome issue or task that you are currently working on in your organization. Choose a problem you care about. Choose a problem you know well enough to allow you to flowchart its process with some detail.

b. Using Post-Its to allow for corrections and flexibility, build a process flowchart for this target process. Include nouns and verbs on each Post-It.

c. Remember, this problem is a current natural consequence of a process in place. You may start by first posting the problem as the last step of the process, and post the preceding steps one at a time moving upstream.

d. Remember to include in your flowchart the processes of current P/R measurements; these feedback
steps occur early (P = preventative) or at the end (R
= result). These steps are posted diagonally to represent questions of, "Are we OK to this point?"

Leading (P) and Lagging (R) indicators

- **P Measurement (process, preventative, proactive, etc):** a feedback measurement which is taken before the last step in a process, and monitored and responded to, can indicate whether a process should be
allowed to continue operating or be stopped to prevent
further errors from being generated. P mechanisms prevent errors by the way they are built.
- **R Measurement (result):** a measurement that is
taken after the last step in a process to confirm the pre
ceding process has generated a success.

2. Document the flowchart's scoreboard.

A scoreboard is a description for the process in question of
"success as measured by..." Here you want the exercise
team to document what they expect a well functioning
process to deliver.

Example:
- **Quality:** complaints on fewer than 5% orders, measur-
able improvement on 75% of our processes.
- **Cost:** operating at or below operating expense plans.
- **Delivery:** delivering product to customers on time 95%
time.
- **Innovation:** supporting two new programs per half
year as outlined in 2007 strategic plan.
- **Safety:** no lost time due to accidents.
- **Employee morale:** employee turnover less than 10%
per year.

- **Revenues, Profit:** maintain 25% profit on results over the month.

3. Flow Chart Bingo procedures

1. Post your troublesome process flow chart on a wall so all team members can see it easily, or on a table in front of you if you are working alone.
2. Confirm that the flow chart represents the process as it currently operates. Correct if necessary.
3. Using colored dots, create a legend with your flowchart's scoreboard that lists its preferred performance. Example: Red = quality, green = cost, yellow = delivery, etc.
4. Review your flowchart; compare each process step with each category of your scoreboard.
5. Place a colored dot wherever you believe a major problem occurs.
6. You will create a map of your process's waste targets.

Dialogue is a conversation that generates learning. Flow Chart Bingo is a dialogue technique that helps to discover which potential problems are located in which segments of a process. The finished flowchart often has a few concentrations of dots and becomes a treasure map. Reducing or eliminating the issues highlighted by the dots will allow the improvement team to accomplish their assigned task.

The history of quality improvement is based on the sequence of these steps: what process is causing the disappointment, what is the standard, what is the gap? Eliminate the gap and pursue the next troublesome process.

FORCE FIELD DIAGRAM

An alternative brainstorming format. Use to identify significant forces which are promoting your success and restraining you from reaching your goals.

Process:

1. Working with team members or others who know the issue best, write a goal at the top of a flip chart.
2. Brainstorm issues which promote the goal, and place them in the left column. Brainstorm issues which restrain the goal and place them in the right column.

GOAL: Implement Improvement Capability

PROMOTING FORCES	RESTRAINING FORCES
customers demanding it	time
company leaders involved	budget
some suppliers can help	last initiative failed
training resources	morale could be better

I like to finish this exercise by ranking each column separately by impact on the project. Confirm you can continue supporting the promoting forces, and assign the highest impact restraining forces to be reduced or eliminated.

PARETO DIAGRAM

This tool helps a team identify the significant few, and the trivial many, when wondering which options to pursue – which are important, which are not. It is often called the 80/20 rule. It seems to describe a principle that has you consider that 80% or your problems come from 20% of your customers, 80% or your revenues come from 20% of your customers, etc.

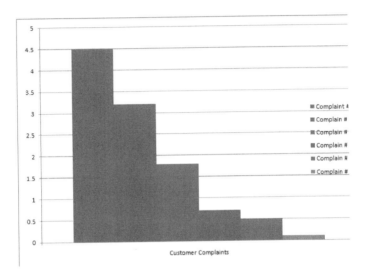

A search of Google Images will provide many examples of this tool's format.

One way to develop a practical Pareto Diagram is to have a team identify a goal, say problems with a team's performance. Have people brainstorm with Post-Its all the possible causes of poor team performance, move them into an affinity diagram, and then take the groups, from the largest group, to the smallest group, and reposition the Post-Its into a stacked bar graph. With the largest group, start with the lower left of a flip chart, and stack all the Post-Its in a tall column.

Then do the same with the next largest group of Post-Its.

Repeat until all the groups are posted.

You have created a Pareto Diagram which shows which cause of poor team performance has the most Post-It entries, and hence the highest bar in the diagram. You would then be encouraged to target the first column's title to work on first to improve a team's performance. The Pareto Diagram encourages you to identify and target the short list of to do's, and not distribute your attention randomly across a wider range of alternatives.

IMPACT EASE DIAGRAM

Use to identify the most significant issue which when improved will provide the most impact with the least effort.

Process:

Collect the list of possible root causes that you want to consider. Construct a two-dimensional matrix to place the selected alternatives in the appropriate "box".

Flip Chart Format

High Impact		
Low Impact		
	Hard to Do	**Easy to Do**

Consider working only with the causes that end up in the upper right corner

WASTE SEARCH

Not too many years ago a manufacturer would have an "acceptable scrap" entry on his balance sheet. This pretty much accepted that waste was inevitable, and to keep it pretty low was a noble goal.

With the advent of teams using tools like process flow charts and improvement processes to really dig into how processes were really being conducted, many forms of waste have come to our attention.

As mentioned earlier, for a company that cannot deliberately improve their processes, this waste is estimated to be 10-30 percent of the organization's revenues. This waste is often hiding in company processes.

"There are many examples of waste in the workplace, but not all waste is obvious. It often appears in the guise of useful work. We must see beneath the surface and grasp the essence."
—Alan Robinson, *Modern Approaches to Manufacturing Improvement*, Productivity Press, 1990.

One of the most famous searchers of waste was Taichii Ohno of Toyota. A significant contribution of Ohno's was his list of the Seven Sources of Waste:

1. Overproduction: too much of the right products or services; extra work.

2. Waiting : delayed action, forgetting.

3. Inventory, Work-in-Process: deteriorating products or services; unused training.

4. Unnecessary Processing : too many steps; no added value.

5. Transportation : excessive time or distance between stations.

6. Motion Within Work Station : in our day-to-day jobs.

7. Defects, Errors.

The key benefit of lists like this is it provides a taxonomy to assist improvement teams in recognizing, understanding, and prioritizing sources of waste. Use Ohno's as you would a Scoreboard in Flowchart Bingo introduced earlier. With the improvement team in attendance looking at a current version of a flowchart, ask, "Do we see any overproduction in this process?"

INTERRELATIONSHIP DIGRAPH

Use to identify and clarify 1) the components of a complex problem, 2) the interrelationships between the components of the problem, and 3) the primary causes of the problem.

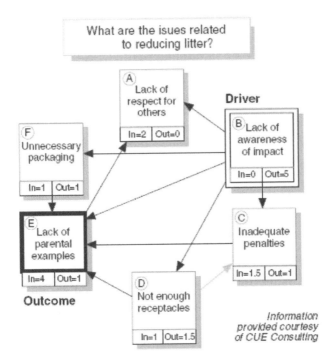

What are the issues related
to reducing litter?

(A) Lack of respect for others | In=2 | Out=0

Driver

(B) Lack of awareness of impact | In=0 | Out=5

(F) Unnecessary packaging | In=1 | Out=1

(E) Lack of parental examples | In=4 | Out=1

Outcome

(C) Inadequate penalties | In=1.5 | Out=1

(D) Not enough receptacles | In=1 | Out=1.5

Information provided courtesy of CUE Consulting

1. Working with people who know the situation, brainstorm cause-components of the problem. Lack of respect, lack of awareness of impact, etc for this example.
2. Arrange causes in a circle on flip chart paper.
3. Draw arrows between all appropriate issue-cards asking, "Which other cards are caused or influenced by this card?" The arrow points from the source of the cause or influence to the result-card in question.
4. The most significant cause has the greatest number of arrows coming from it; the best indicator of success has the most arrows going into it.

PRIORITIZING PROCESS

- Scoreboard
- Brainstorming
- Multivoting
- Decision Matrix

One of my favorite sequences of decision-making exercises that promotes and provokes dialogue is Scoreboard, Brainstorm, Multivote and Decision Matrix. This may sound complicated but really it's quite easy.

You have read about the Scoreboard and Brainstorming tools earlier.

1. To complete the next two steps, Multivote and Decision Matrix, post all the possible root causes you want to consider on a flip chart. Meet at a flip chart stand or flip chart on a wall and present and discuss each idea one at a time. Each person presents one of their ideas as it is their turn. Sell your idea in terms of the scoreboard criteria. Promote dialogue. Dialogue should include people with data clarifying how a particular car does or does not fulfill criteria from the scoreboard. If you weren't sure, you'd suspend the meeting, and go find out. Data drives the dialogue, not opinion.

2. Multivote: if you end up with more than six options to choose from, quickly narrow the list by having people vote for their favorite options. Give everyone ten votes but stipulate they cannot put any more than five votes on any one option. Vote, tabulate, and take the four high scorers to the next step.

3. After multivoting, select the best choice with the use of a decision matrix: using a five point impact scale: 5 = great fit, 1 = poor fit. Here you compare each pair/cell. So Choice A, how does it support quality? Team

discussion = 4. How does Choice B support quality?
Team discussion = 3, and so on.

Decision Matrix:

	Choice A	Choice B	Choice C	Choice D
Quality	4	3	4	5
Cost	2	4	5	3
Practical	4	3	2	3
Safety	4	2	3	4
Fun	5	4	3	2
TOTAL	19	16	17	17

While the four choices are close, if you can agree to support Choice A as the best fit, this collaborative process has helped you make a good decision with good support.

Step 4 should end with the improvement team eager to revise their assigned process, ready to conduct an experiment to confirm their best guesses as to the significant root causes.

Step 5. PLAN: MODIFY FLOW CHART

Step 5 has the improvement team analyze what they have learned in the previous steps and develop their best guess of what an improved flow chart would look like.

PROCESS FLOW CHART WITH P/R MEASUREMENTS

Using a new flip chart and Post-Its (do not cannibalize your earlier version of the current assigned process) develop a flowchart whose process will meet or exceed the criteria outlined in the scoreboard. Place P and R measures (feedback loops) where they will help.

There are a number of helpful lists to prompt an improvement team to consider particular improvement strategies. For example, use the Harrington list below when it's time to improve the current process. With the improvement team in attendance looking at a current version of a flowchart, ask, "Can we improve our process by eliminating bureaucracy?"

Another taxonomy useful with service producing processes:

Twelve Cornerstone Tools – Improvement Recommendations

1. Bureaucracy Elimination: unnecessary administrative tasks
2. Duplication Elimination: identical activities
3. Value-added assessment: contributes to customer expectations
4. Simplification: reduce complexity
5. Process Cycle-Time Reduction: shorten cycles
6. Error-Proofing : Poka Yoke
7. Upgrading: effective use of capital
8. Simple Language: easy for user to comprehend
9. Standardization: selecting a single way
10. Supplier Partnerships: improve inputs
11. Big Picture Improvement: systems view
12. Automation and/or Mechanization: free up people from routine tasks

—Dr. H.J. Harrington, *Business Process Improvement: The Breakthrough Strategy for Total Quality, Productivity, and Competitiveness,*, McGraw-Hill, 1991

BENCHMARK

Benchmarking, in a business sense, is about comparing your own organization to "the best." How do you measure up compared to the winners? And specifically, with an improvement team assigned a troublesome process, what can the team learn from other organizations with similar processes that would provide ideas to include in a modified flowchart?

While wanting to differentiate my organization, and not just "be as good as x," benchmarking is also a method to help improvement and innovation teams to "discover what's possible."

With the helpful mental model of a process flow chart, you are on a treasure hunt for more efficient and effective process flow chart steps and leading and lagging indicators

Process:

It is best to do this work with a team that knows their own processes well, is willing to learn from other process owners, in and out of their company, and likes developing the output to this process up on a wall with lots of flip charts and Post-Its.

1. Identify macro-processes key to success
2. Build a macro flow chart of your company.
3. Analyze and prioritize key macro-processes
4. Select the processes which improved would provide the greatest impact to your organization as measured by your Scoreboard.
5. Identify key micro-processes

6. Build micro flow charts of the processes selected in Step Two.
7. Identify key metrics for each micro process
8. Identify and document key P/R measurements (leading, lagging indicators)
9. Identify potential sources of information
10. What other organizations, in and out of your industry, might exercise a process that you are studying much better than you do? Who can possibly show you "what's possible?"
11. Determine how benchmarks will be collected.
12. Plan your treasure hunt by securing or building flow-charts of the process you will investigate. List your questions before you go. Make arrangements to tour with people who really know the process.
13. Collect the data.
14. Use appropriate means to capture what you see: flow charts, run charts, histograms, procedures, videos, testimonials, etc.
15. Analyze the data.
16. Establish improvement goals and action plans.
17. PDCA on process changes.
18. Treat data as you would using your organization's improvement process
19. Incorporate benchmarking into planning.
20. Proactively feed your strategic and tactical planning by selecting tasks in reference to company Scoreboards, industry benchmarks, etc.
21. Keep looking over your shoulder.

Be open to learning about improvements wherever you may be.

—adapted from *American Samurai,* by William Lareau (Grand Central Publishing, 1992)

LEADERSHIP Buy Off #1 OF 2

This is the first of two buy offs.

At this point the improvement team confirms for a representative of the L&GT that the team's proposed flow chart will fulfill or exceed the success criteria documented in the improvement team's scoreboard.

Once the flow chart has been modified and is ready for a trial run, a representative of the L&GT should meet with the team leader, and possibly the team, to provide a buy off to moving ahead. Best case this representative of the L&GT has been monitoring the improvement team's Storyboard regularly since the improvement team's start. At any point during the work of the first five steps if this leader has any questions, concerns, or suggestions they will immediately contact the improvement team leader to work the issue. Do not wait till later. When this L&GT representative monitors the improvement team on an ongoing basis they are prepared to give the improvement team a buy off during this buy off meeting, not a few weeks later when more data is collected or other questions are answered. Besides accelerating the implementation of the improvement, this immediate decision is a morale booster to the improvement team

---

Step 6. DO: TRY OUT IMPROVEMENTS

In Step Six, the improvement team conducts an experiment with the new modified process. This experiment should be as similar as possible to the real world situation it will be running once it is transferred to the team where the new process will be run.

PROCESS FLOW CHART WITH P/R MEASUREMENTS

The assigned process improved in Step Five will be documented with a revised process flowchart and appropriate P and R measures (feedback loops).

CHECK SHEET AND RUN CHART

Data should be collected and formatted in check sheets or run charts to show that the results of the improved process results meet or exceed the Scoreboard criteria.

PROCESS DECISION PROGRAM CHART

I prefer that the improvement team consider how they will transfer their improved process to the group that will be using the improved process in such a way that the new group can and wants to succeed with the improved process.

Consider the difference between an installation and an implementation. An installation has an improvement team revise a process and "throw it over the wall" to the receiving team. "We did our best, here it is, now it's your responsibility." An implementation has the improvement team responsible for the transfer of capability. So whatever needs to be done to allow the receiving team to successfully maintain the improved process is part of the improvement team's tasks. A Process Decision Program Chart is a very good way to discuss and plan for anything that might hinder a successful transfer of the improved process from the improvement team to the receiving team. The process decision program chart is a planning tool used to identify and arrange the steps of a project's process steps and sub steps, anticipate the possible problems and consequences of the steps, and consider proactive responses to possible problems. It is a form of scenario thinking.

Process:

1. Assemble the improvement team with the team which will be affected by the process.
2. Identify the process and document with a macro process flow chart of the improved process.
3. Continue by documenting second-level steps.
4. Then wonder aloud about what might go wrong and list as "what ifs."
5. Then together decide on possible reactions to the what ifs.

Arrange in the following format:

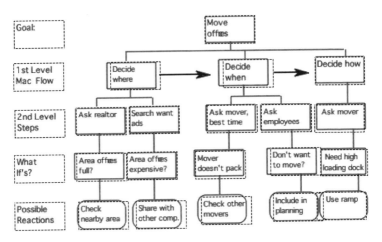

The benefit of the conversation that builds this diagram is that the team wonders about and addresses issues before they happen. So not only is this thinking done in a less emotional context, i.e. more rational, it also helps team members both recognize and react to the what-ifs far sooner than they would if they hadn't spent the time thinking about it.

Step 7. CHECK: STUDY RESULTS

The purpose of Step Seven is to allow any parties that have a contribution to make, at least the improvement team and the receiving team, to confirm the proposed improvement process actually delivered what the process was designed to do.

- Check Sheet
- Run Chart
- Histogram
- Charter
- Scoreboard

All of the above tools can be used to document the results of the experiment conducted with the proposed improved process.

SHOW ME THE MONEY

I do recommend the improvement team does work with a member of the organization's finance team to confirm that the work to date will likely deliver the intended results as measured by a more in depth look by people with the skills to "dollarize" the benefit of the Improved Process.

LEADERSHIP Buy Off #2 OF 2

This is the second of two buy offs.

At this point the improvement team confirms for a representative of the L&GT that the team's proposed flow chart does fulfill or exceed the success criteria documented in the improvement team's Scoreboard. The improvement team's Storyboard should include the data and analysis to support this position. This buy off then allows the improvement team to transfer the Improved Process to the receiving team and disband this improvement team after completing steps 8-10.

Step 8. ACT: STANDARDIZE IMPROVEMENTS

- Collaboration Skills
- Customer Research
- Systematic Diagram
- Process Decision Program Chart
- Gantt Chart

The purpose of Step Eight is for the improvement team to work with the receiving team to fully implement the Improved Process successfully.

Step 9. PLAN: PLAN NEXT IMPROVEMENTS

- Purpose, Vision, Goals, Etc.
- Leading Change
- Customer Research
- Scoreboard
- Establish Team

Many organizations have the improvement team which is about to be disbanded to spend one meeting talking about what they learned and to recommend other processes for improvement. I recommend that the current improvement team is disbanded and another improvement team be formed to support additional assigned processes. This would start with the work of the L&GT as described earlier. As mentioned before, I encourage this team to think about their improvement teams as spectacular investment opportunities.

Considering that a team can reduce the expenses in a targeted process by 10-30%, often with little or no capital, the improvement teams succeeding can be thought of as one of the primary money makers in an organization. It warrants and deserves their full attention and support.

5
Introduce Creative Thinking Skills

Chapters five and six will help you build skills to be more creative in a business sense (vs. artistic), to develop the ability to deliberately generate additional useful insights and ideas. Innovation is the ability to select, combine, refine, and turn the best creative ideas into reality, revenues, and profits. Successful companies have learned how to exercise both skill sets.

	Tactical	Strategic
Improve (Convergent)	Process Improvement Skills	Strategic Planning
	Collaboration Skills	
Innovate (Divergent)	Creative Thinking Skills	Scenario Planning

Where - The Phenomenon of Creativity

Our brains are wonderful data storage and retrieval systems which prefer patterns and repetition. They recognize new ideas that are similar enough to recorded ideas so they "fit" into the pre-existing collection. Truly new ideas often don't even register in this hierarchy of set patterns. It also seems that truly new ideas often come from the "accidental" crossing of paradigms, mixing new ideas that just don't logically belong together.

The self-organizing capacity of our brains goes to work on this new, unique combination and tries tirelessly to "make sense" of the novel combination. "Lots of ideas" is the wonderful byproduct; 90% will be thrown away, but 10% will often include ideas, never before conceived, which warrant further consideration. Our brain is willing and able to make unusual combinations between seemingly unrelated words, ideas, pictures, etc. It likes to "free associate," as we like to day dream. One idea leads to another which makes me think of another ideas which reminds me about..."Hey, where did you come up with that crazy idea, anyway?"

How (continued from the earlier conversation about growing dendrites in chapter 2)

While there are many myths about creativity (creative people are always artists, or nerds, or not like you and me, etc.), a modern understanding of creativity recognizes techniques are available to assist anyone who knows how to use them. Effective creativity techniques deliberately mix up paradigms while addressing real problems and opportunities to proactively generate lots of new ideas. These techniques do not need to depend on chance occurrences. These techniques can be used at will whenever individuals or teams recognize they need more ideas. "Creative people" learn to recognize they may have to use an illogical technique to generate what they will only later come to recognize and appreciate as a logical alternative. Go figure!

The effective use of creative thinking skills will provide the precipitating events discussed earlier. Dr. David Perkins, author of *Archimedes' Bathtub: The Art and Logic of Breakthrough Thinking,* offers a five-step structure that describes breakthrough thinking:

1. Long Search: Breakthrough thinking requires time and effort.

2. Little Apparent Progress: A typical breakthrough arrives after little or no apparent progress.

3. Precipitating Event: The typical breakthrough begins with a precipitating event. Sometimes external circumstances cue this moment.

4. Cognitive Snap: The breakthrough comes rapidly, kind of falling into place, a cognitive snap. Not much time separates the precipitating event from the solution even if details remain to be checked.

5. Transformation: The breakthrough transforms one's mental or physical world in a generative way.

Creativity - A Phenomenon – Precipitating Events: Stepping Stones

Dr. Edward de Bono calls these tools stepping stones. Example tools include Analogies, Imaginary Brainstorming, Random Word, and Biotechnique. These will be described in chapter six.

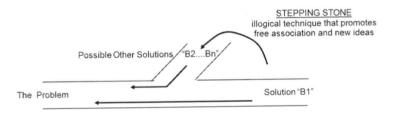

De Bono presents the phenomenon in the following way. Solution "B1" is an obvious solution to the problem. Using illogical techniques, solution "B2...Bn", which may be unique and innovative, can be generated. And when new B's are compared to the goal, they are often (another junk drawer) deemed useful.

The concept of a stepping stone is fundamental. I need to look at an opportunity from another point to see something in a different way. I cannot prejudge whether I'll like the new view until after I try it. When I look at something in a new way my brain will quickly offer all sorts of new combinations and ideas. Keep shaking that Magic Eight ball, looking for answers.

Stepping stones can be anywhere: from creative thinking techniques to unusual books, movies, thinkers, hardware stores, museums, travels, walks, naps, games, etc. Anything that at least temporarily changes your point of view is a stepping stone to new combinations and insights.

Effective creative thinking always encourages one to at least try the new point of view before making any decisions. The purpose of effective techniques is to provide new useful stepping stones to promote "precipitating events."

Considerations About Thinking

Herbert Benson, M.D., and William Proctor write about similar phenomenon to Perkin's five-step model in their book *Break Out Principle*. They talk about peak experiences, including creative events, which often occur in four stages:

1. Hard struggle.
2. Letting go.
3. Breakout event with peak experience; with surprise.
4. Return to new normal higher state.

An individual's triggers are those activities which help a person to change their mental and emotional patterns completely and move more deliberately to Step Three, the breakout event. This is very similar to Perkin's precipitating event leading to a cognitive snap.

Benson and Proctor provide a list of characteristics of effective triggers, including repetitious and engaging. The time it takes for a trigger to work will vary with individuals and often requires at least fifteen minutes. Triggers which assist letting go:

- Religion
- Music
- Cultural events
- Art
- Reading and listening to spoken word
- Water (shower, tub, hot tub, etc)
- Rest room (shaving, grooming, etc)
- Athletic (jogging, walking, bicycling, etc)
- Watching items closely (staring at items)
- House work (washing dishes, gardening, repairing items, etc)
- Surrender triggers (letting go)
- Restaurants (quiet dinner with trusted person)

- Time with pets (petting, talking, etc)
- Altruistic (helping others)
- Brainstorming with teams

—From *The Break-out Principle*, by Herbert Benson, M.D., and William Proctor

I mention this here to recommend that you consider the environment and process you use to most predictably generate new ideas. Learn what works for you.

To Be Creative – Strategy Alternatives

New ideas can come to people accidentally, when they expect them least. When we want new ideas, we're pleasantly surprised when this happens.

New ideas can also come to people with the use of a structured process. This approach attempts to duplicate the conditions necessary for new ideas to occur. Using a good, creative ideation process allows people to be creative on purpose.

I do want to distinguish between two approaches to creative thinking skills. One strategy would suggest all you need to do is change your environment. Externally turn the lights down, play some soft music, sit on the floor, just relax. And internally stop thinking about troublesome issues and the ideas will flow. The hard-liners for this strategy believe that creative process is an oxymoron.

Another strategy discussed earlier says that ideas are the result of provoking the brain's axons with great questions. When the brain is actively and deliberately engaged this way, you are likely to find new ideas (dendrites) coming to your mind.

While I think one can engage and enjoy both

strategies, I much prefer the second when I really have to come up with some ideas on demand. Just relaxing takes so much time, with little apparent progress.

Why Bother, and How - Considerations About Creativity and Innovation

In the Dec. 5, 2005 Resilience Report from Booz Allen Hamilton, more evidence that you can't spend your way to innovation prosperity. The results of the Booz Allen study of the Global Innovation 1000 (the thousand public companies that spend the most on R&D), challenge the traditional notion that to increases in R&D budgets equate to successful innovation results. Major findings from the survey:

"Money doesn't buy results. There is no relationship between R&D spending and the primary measures of economic or corporate success, such as growth, enterprise profitability, and shareholder return.

"It's the process, not the pocketbook. Superior results, in most cases, seem to be a function of the quality of an organization's innovation process — the bets it makes and how it pursues them — rather than the magnitude of its innovation spending.

"Collaboration is key. The link between spending and performance tends to be strongest in those areas most under the control of the R&D silo, such as product design, and weakest in those areas where cross-functional collaboration is most difficult, such as commercialization.

Personally, I take this as great confirmation that the agile and creative among us can win against the big guys.

To repeat Toyota's Chairman Dr. Cho, "Brilliant

process management is our strategy. We get brilliant results from average people managing brilliant processes. We observe that our competitors often get average (or worse) results from brilliant people managing broken processes."

To Innovate or Not Innovate – The Cost of Waiting

Ideally, a company wants to change, improve, i.e. learn, faster than its competitors. It may well be the rate at which a company learns that will differentiate it from its competitors.

Delaying learning can contribute to unnecessary costs. If I could learn to improve a $1,000,000 (operating cost) process and reduce its expenses only 10% (industry numbers suggest an unimproved process is likely generating 10-30% waste), I spend an additional $8,400 for each month I delay the improvement, $25,000 for each quarter, $100,000 for each year.

Delaying a new product introduction, which is targeted to generate $5,000,000 annually will cost $416,000 for each delayed month in lost revenue. Delaying the same new product introduction one year will cost $8,745,000 over the course of five years assuming a 15%. growth rate.

Deciding not to do something can be very expensive.

6
Practice Creative Thinking Skills

Creative Thinking Skills Process Steps – Introduction (Macro View)

An example Creative Thinking Skills Process might look like this:

1. Select goal and success criteria, and describe current situation
2. Generate ideas
3. Select Ideas
4. Implement Ideas

Comparing this process with the improvement process in chapters three and four, creative thinking kills is mostly about divergent ideas, more ideas when I have too few. Process improvement is mostly about finding possible root cause in a process. This is a convergent search for causes, I want to reduce the number of causes to deal with before I modify my assigned process.

As with the improvement team, creative teams can benefit from doing much of their work together to all to hear and build on each others' ideas. Room set up is the same, using Post-Its and working on the wall is the same.

There are many books available to help you learn to be more creative deliberately. The one I have used most often in client situations is The Creativity Tools Memory Jogger: A Pocket Guide for Creative Thinking by Michael Brassard and Diane Ritter (1998; www.goalqpc.com).

Creative Thinking Skills Process Steps and Tools (Mini View)

1. Select Goal and Success Criteria.
- Big Picture.
- Goal Statement.
- Scoreboard.
- Large-Scale Diagram.

2a. Generate Ideas – Tier One.
- Brainstorming with Post-Its.
- Brainwriting 6-3-5.
- Mind Mapping.

2b. Generate Ideas – Tier Two.
- Word Associations.
- Analogies.
- Imaginary Brainstorming.
- Picture Associations and Biotechniques.

3. Select Ideas .
- Idea Box.
- Prioritizing (with Scoreboard, Multivoting, and Decision Matrix).
- TILMAG.

4. Implement Ideas
- Leading Change

Creative Thinking Skills Process Steps and Tools (Micro View)

Step 1. Select goal and success criteria, and describe current situation.

Big Picture, Goal Statement, Scoreboard, Large Scale Diagram. You have seen a very similar series of tools in Chapter 4, Improvement Process Step Three, Plan, Describe Current Situation, Gather Data.

Fundamentally, the first step in the Creative Process is all about building alignment and synergy around the starting point for any team setting out to generate ideas. As a team they are heading out on a scavenger hunt for great ideas. You are trying to provoke dialogue, to have a robust conversation about what you need to target and know in order to generate a useful alternative. The more they share clarity about the purpose, success criteria, and the limits of their search, the more productive they will be. Your workspace for a team should be a conference room with lots of wall space, plenty of markers, flip charts, Post-Its, tape, etc to let you easily document your conversations and progress.

Select Goal:

This first step and question asks the team what do they want to accomplish. A great new product, or a great new office location, or a great new engineer, etc. The selection of the goal statement is important. It will direct the creative team about what to look for. A key consideration is scope. While one goal statement might read, "Reduce expenses in a particular site," another from the same team might read, "Improve revenues in our organization." Considered alongside each other, reducing expenses can be seen as a strategy for improving revenues. And yet a team may, in fact, have been given or chosen the narrower statement. I have found broader statements more useful in generating a wider variety of ideas. Knowing what level to target is part of the art of this process. This comes with experience.

Success Criteria:

I like to define the preferred state of the goal very clearly with a scoreboard. Just what do we really want to accomplish? When we have found a creative solution, what will it fulfill? If possible, the scoreboard will include categories and numbers. So "improving quality, cost, and delivery" is better than "improve revenues," and "improving quality to 150 DPM, cost to $2.50 per item and delivery to one day" are even better. The clearer the finish line, the easier it is for the team to know what they're working towards and to recognize when they're done.

Understand the Current Situation:

In fancy words, you're trying to "understand the system that surrounds the opportunity." When a team assembles for the first time to develop creative ideas, they likely have a wide variety of perceptions about just what is going on in the situation that includes the opportunity statement. It is very helpful to diagram what you are learning as you learn it. Here's an example. Imagine prospective homebuilders talking to their architect. This conversation would be frustrating without diagrams to demonstrate ideas in sufficient detail for the listener to understand the speaker's intent. These diagrams in your own work situation can have many forms: relationship diagrams, process flow charts, mind maps, workflow diagrams, anything that makes it easy for people to share and understand ideas.

- **Relationship Diagram:** show how the respective individuals/departments work in a matrix of relationships.
- **Process Flow Chart:** this document will show the sequence of the steps to complete.
- **Value Chain** shows columns of respective vertical processes allowing for appropriate connections between the processes.
- **Workflow Diagram** shows how people are moving around in the work area.

It is also crucial that these diagrams describe current reality, with all its warts. This step is best done with the help of trips to the site of the situation in question. Don't settle for, "As I remember it." Get into the factories to see the issues, talk with customers in the buying place to see their issues, talk to experts about the marketplace. In other words, gather data. It people disagree about the situation they are describing, ask questions that provide the data that clears up what's really happening in the given situation.

These three tasks of the first step of the creative process can be improved as the dialogue continues. The goal statement, scoreboard, and diagram can be revised at any time to assist the team members in achieving their purpose.

Step 2a. Generate Ideas – Tier One

- Brainstorming with Post-Its:
- Brainwriting 6-3-5
- Mind Mapping:

The purpose of Step 2a is to develop a good list of potential solutions to your goal statement.

Generating Ideas - Considerations

You've been here before. "Let's have some ideas," "Let's brainstorm."

Merriam Webster describes brainstorming as, "A group problem-solving tool that involves the spontaneous contribution of ideas from all members of the group." Coming up with new ideas can be hard work. Time, focus, and discipline seem to be often necessary. This book's process and its tools make it easier. Using a series of tools to generate ideas is like going to a store, an "Ideas R Us," a huge warehouse of great ideas. Each time we head down a new aisle, we're using another tool. Any idea we like that occurs to us while we use the tool, we grab it and put it into our shopping cart. A few aisles and tools later, we're at checkout with way too many ideas, so we have to select the best—great problem to have.

Generating Ideas – Tier One and Tier Two Tools

I use two tiers of brainstorming tools:

- **Tier One:** Brainstorming with Post-Its, 6-3-5, and Mindmapping.
- **Tier Two:** Word Associations, Analogies, Imaginary Brainstorming, and Picture Associations and Biotools.

These of course are only examples of the two tiers. There are likely hundreds of tools available to help you come up with ideas.

Tier One tools generate more and similar ideas. Tier One tools ask you to think about associations and ideas that come to mind. This is common brainstorming.

Tier Two tools generate fewer and more unusual ideas. Tier Two tools ask you to think about associations not associated with your project which then can provoke you to generate unusual ideas. This is Yenta at work (see chapter two). This is less common brainstorming.

Please notice as we progress through the simpler tools and into the more unusual tools that the quantity and uniqueness of your ideas will change. In my experience, if I'm really looking for a truly new idea, I do need to do the work of clearing my radar screen of current ideas to make room for new ideas.

Complete at least two rounds of Tier One brainstorming before going to Tier Two. If I were to move to the more unusual tools first, I would likely not end up with newer ideas but rather the ones I've been thinking about recently.

Brainstorming with Post-Its

There are many ways to brainstorm for ideas. One common process has a facilitator/scribe write down ideas as participants call them out. Common ground rules are "no bad ideas," one person at a time, anything goes, etc. Choose a process that generates lots of good ideas and group excitement.

Having conducted many many idea generating sessions, I have found it most useful to have team members document "ideas" individually on 3" x 3" Post-It's. As in Step One, your workspace for a team should be a conference room with lots of wall space, plenty of markers, flip charts, Post-Its, tape, etc., to let you easily document your conversations and progress.

My preferred process has the participants starting a session sitting at a table, clarifying the goal statement, the initiative's scoreboard, and Big Picture diagram's messages. Then each participant silently writes down their own ideas for solutions (ideas to fulfill the opportunity statement) on their Post-It pad with a non-permanent, pencil-size marker, one idea per Post-It sheet. Write large enough so people can read each idea from a distance. All participants are writing on their pads at the same time; the room is quiet. This goes on for about five minutes.

Then to debrief the ideas the participants stand in a semicircle at a flip chart titled "Brainstorming," and share their ideas with each other. Each person presents and sells (sharing how their idea fulfills the scoreboard) their first idea to the group. Then you repeat this process until all ideas have been presented. One person at a time, one idea at a time. This balances participation. Place all the ideas on Post-Its on the flip chart. No need to organize them here. You could stack the duplicate ideas to show a number of people liked this idea.

Remembering that dialogue can describe the kind of conversation that builds a synergistic new and better understanding of an issue, this should be a very chatty session. These conversations also provide an opportunity for additional ideas to be discussed and posted.

Considering that brainstorming is about coming up with ideas, remember the value of a junk drawer. Pictures of related ideas posted on the wall, boxes of cool stuff placed all over the work table, tours of the related work/ customer areas, speakers with different points of view, etc., all stimulate new ideas. Have your Post-It pads with you anytime you're near a good junk drawer.

This method of brainstorming, including the Post-Its, the time alone to come up with your own ideas, the one-idea-at-a-time presentation of ideas to me is the key to the success of this method. The Post-Its, the flip chart, the neutral place to look when you're placing and discussing the Post-Its, and the process are a great leveler—letting quiet people come up with their ideas and knowing they have a chance to present and be heard, and the noisy people to take a minute to think before talking, and not being allowed to dominate the conversation.

I think of Post-Its and flip charts as the currency of dialogue. More complicated technology-based alternatives do not provide the same success.

Brainwriting 6 - 3 - 5

This is another way to brainstorm. The title comes from: six people, working to generate three ideas in each five minute exercise.

This exercise is best done quietly allowing each member to collect and document their own thoughts. You start in row 1, listing your three ideas. Five minutes goes by. You pass your sheet to the next person. They now have the chance to come up with their own ideas or piggyback off yours.

Process:

1. Assemble the team and clarify the issue.
2. Complete the 6-3-5 worksheets; sheets with arranged Post-Its.
3. Analyze the ideas and select the best ones.
4. Use nominal group technique to debrief.

Sample 6 – 3 – 5: Six people, generating three ideas, during each five minute round:

Employee Recognition Options

Round/ Person	Idea # 1	Idea # 2	Idea # 3
1	Pizza coupons	Movie coupons	Shopping coupons
2	Potluck at work	Picnic at area park	Wall of fame
3	Video of work highlighted	Letter from president	Day off from work
4	Winner presents to company	Letter from work team	Day off to volunteer
5	Winner presents to suppliers	Thank you letter to spouse	Dinner coupons
6	Surprise dinner from workteam	News clip sent to local news	News clip to tv station

Arrows represent ideas that came from piggy backing off the earlier ideas.

I recommend that teams start off with a large paper sheet with as many rows as there are team members, and three columns for the three ideas per person. In each of these cells, place a blank Post-It. The advantage here is to have all you ideas in the same format, on Post-Its, so when it's time to narrow your selections, you can walk past all the tools you used and their flip charts, and easily pick the ideas you want to recommend for further consideration.

Mind Mapping

Tony Buzan (author of *The Mind Map Book* and numerous other titles) gets the credit for this helpful technique. It looks like a multidimensional org chart with an idea in each one of the boxes, but a lot messier.

Start with the group facing a wall with 2-3 flip charts taped together onto the wall to make for one large, open work surface. Writing with letters about an inch high, start with a circle in the center and write the goal statement text inside. Then, silently, each participant armed with their own pen-sized markers, has at it writing new ideas right on the flip chart paper that answer the question, "How can we fulfill the goal statement?" Same question as in brainstorming but using a very different approach to post the ideas.

This looks like a frenzied freshman ride board at college, everybody writing away at the same time, moving every once in a while to work on another area of the map. Ten minutes ought to do it. But if people are still working, don't stop them. The debrief is similar to brainstorming; as you review the sea of circles/ideas, when it's your turn, pick an idea, rewrite it on a Post-It, cover the idea on the map and sell it to your scoreboard. New ideas are always welcome.

Coming up with new ideas can be hard work. Done well, this is a lot of fun and very productive. A good ideation process and its techniques make it easier. Brainstorming with Post-Its and 6-3-5 are good for quieter groups who may just be starting their work together, mind mapping is good for more gregarious groups who have lots of ideas they want to share quickly.

To maintain the format of ideas to be on Post-Its, it's best to copy the best ideas onto Post-Its after the mind map is complete. This is more of a group exercise with everyone writing on the same sheet of flip chart paper at the same time. Post-Its also take up too much space here.

1. Write the topic (or draw a picture that represents it) in the center or extreme side of a sizable piece of paper.
2. Brainstorm ideas around the topic. For each major idea, draw a line directly from the main topic.
3. For each new idea, decide whether it is a new theme or a variation on an existing idea. Record ideas on the lines as they are generated.
4. Continue thinking, drawing, and recording until the ideas (or the people involved) are exhausted.

5. Asking "How can we do that?" while looking at an idea helps you come up with additional ideas.

6. To debrief as with the previous tools, go around the circle of team members one at a time. Find an idea you like on the charts and duplicate the idea onto a Post-Its, placing it over the idea you duplicated.

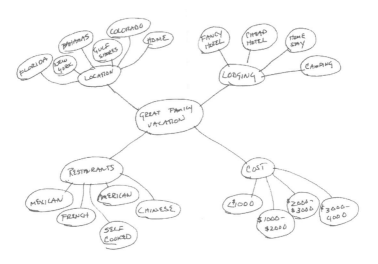

Step 2b.Generate Ideas – Tier Two
- Word Associations
- Analogies
- Imaginary Brainstorming
- Picture Associations and Biotechniques

"Wow, neat idea. Where did that come from?" We all have come up with unusual new ideas in the past. Many do this accidentally. Some can do it more easily than others. I hope to help you learn how to do it on purpose.

To introduce you to what this is like, try this at home. Have someone take five note sheets and write the numbers "1, 2, 3..." on one sheet, "A,B,C,..." on a second sheet, and then a different random word (animals, fruits, places, etc) on sheets 3, 4, and 5.

Have your helper then ask you, "What comes to mind when I show you these notes one at a time?" Have them lead with "1,2,3" and "A,B,C," then follow with the three random words. If you've grown up on this planet and gone to school, you will most likely respond "4, 5, 6..." to the numbered note, "D, E, F..." to the lettered note. But when you are shown a random word and asked what comes to mind, your response is likely dissimilar to another person's response.

The point of this exercise is to demonstrate what many call "free association." Our responses to "123" and "ABC" show us how patterned or convergent thinking works. Our less likely responses to the random words show us how unpatterned or divergent thinking works. The point to appreciate here is that this happens. We will very likely have some response to the random reference that could explain how we came to it. Without the word to stimulate our thinking and response, we will likely just sit—you can't will yourself a new idea. New ideas are provoked.

Let's say I'm wondering, "How can I move fast food along a kitchen assembly line?" For Tier Two (Random Word) we somehow come up with the word "kiwi." Team members brainstorm any word that occurs to them as they consider the word kiwi. Responses might include, tasty, small, rolls, fuzzy, or expensive.

If we stop here, there is no progress, just frustration. So luckily we know to ask, while considering the associations one-by-one, "How does this word association help me develop a practical solution to my opportunity statement?" (Practical solutions get listed on Post-Its as did previous practical solutions from Brainstorming and Mind Mapping.)

Consider "fuzzy." How does fuzzy help me come up with a practical solution to moving fast food in a kitchen assembly line? From out of nowhere comes an idea from your experience. You may remember the fuzzy legs on the bottom of the football or soccer player figures of a children's tabletop game where the board vibrated and the players moved in the direction they had been set up. And you're thinking, "Hey that could work—we could have a vibrating surface that orders would be placed on and they would move toward checkout." Notice that the perceived value of the idea occurs after you have completed the exercise.

Now this may not be a $10 million idea right out of the chute, but this new idea was not on any list we had in the Tier One Brainstorming exercises. It is new and considerable, contributing to a more interesting junk drawer. When you know how to think this way you can do this on purpose. You can also use all sorts of random things besides words: sounds and pictures for example. There are many other Tier Two tools with structured processes to help you do this regularly.

SO WHAT?

Tier Two Brainstorming tools take you to another point of view. In looking back at your opportunity statement you will likely see very different practical ideas than you would have if you only surrounded yourself with the familiar and ordinary points of view. To my experience, the result of this and similar processes is what people mean when they talk about thinking outside the box. To do this accidentally or deliberately, you now have a choice.

Singing songs that we know is easier than making them up, and someone might not like the new ones. Here's the rub though: innovation is built on new ideas. When teams can appreciate they will want to use what may seem to be illogical techniques like random word to provoke new associations and to generate ideas they will come to respect as logical alternatives. Then they know how to think to fuel innovation on purpose.

Word Associations (Random Word)

The fundamental principle here is to use a random reference point to generate ideas. A random point will most likely take you down a different thought path (associations). You then generate ideas around the central problem itself (practical ideas). The random reference point can be a word, object, picture, etc. The key is to make it random. For example take the second reading from a watch and chose that number from a list of sixty words.

Use the random word, object, etc. to open up new ideas around the chosen problem.

1. Define the problem clearly and brainstorm initial ideas.
2. Determine the source and select stimulating words to use.
3. Brainstorm *associations* that are stimulated by the selected word.
4. Take the ideas identified in Step 3 and restate them as *practical ideas* as they apply to the problem.

Repeat the process as often as is helpful, using a new word each time. Pool the best ideas.

Example:

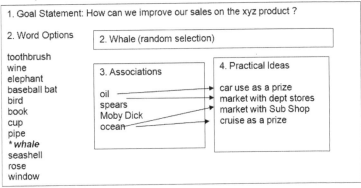

Analogies

The purpose of this tool is to discover if there are similar situations that would be useful to compare to the problem at hand. You then generate ideas around the central problem itself (practical ideas).

The random reference point can be a word, object, picture, etc. The key is to make it random. For example take the second reading from a watch and chose that number from a list of sixty words.

In this case, substitute the problem under consideration with analogies that have similar dynamics. For example, how could a child improve the sales for her lemonade stand, or a Girl Scout sell more cookies, or a real estate agent more houses, etc.

1. Define the problem clearly and brainstorm initial ideas.

2. Brainstorm analogies that are stimulated by the selected word. Consider your analogy while wondering what is the key concept in your practical situation.
3. Take the ideas identified in Step Two and restate them as practical ideas as they apply to the problem.

Imaginary Brainstorming

1. Define the essential elements of the problem or goal statement: subject, verb, object.
2. Propose imaginary replacements for one of the elements of the problem statement. It is easiest to start with the subject. One helpful characteristic of the subject is that it has to be able to think, to have a point of view. Wilder is better; wilder takes you to a stepping stone that you have not exercised before. Select by number of laughs.
3. Formulate a new problem statement, substituting one of the imaginary elements. After you get good at substituting subjects, then try objects, then both.
4. Brainstorm the new subject's solutions. Magic Eight Ball! Be sure to listen to your imagination and record what it offers you.
5. And now to make it practical: apply ideas from the imaginary brainstorming back to the real problem statement.
6. Analyze all of the brainstormed ideas (real, imaginary, combined) and further explore the more interesting ones.

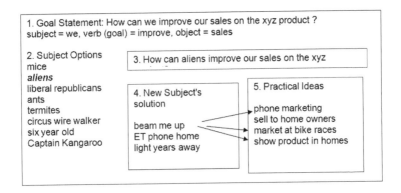

Picture Associations and Biotechniques

In Picture Associations, you substitute photos for random words. How does the photo stimulate your thinking? What associations occur as a result of considering the photo?

In Biotechniques, you substitute living organisms for random words. How does the consideration of a living organism stimulate your thinking? What associations occur as a result of considering the life form? How would they solve this problem, achieve this goal or similar goal?

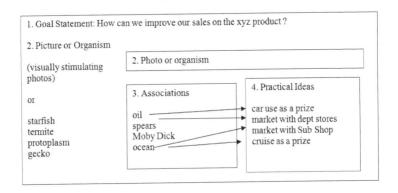

Use the random photo, living organism, etc., to open up new ideas around the chosen problem.

Tier Two Brainstorming Review

My hope is that the previous Tier Two exercises have increased your tolerance for, even encouragement of, silly thinking and the associated laughter. This thinking and behavior do have their place in an organization that's truly serious about nurturing new ideas. New ideas that produce new products and services, that produce new revenues and profitability.

3. Select Ideas

- Idea Box
- Prioritizing (with Scoreboard, Multivoting, and Decision Matrix)
- TILMAG

Decision Making - Preparation

To this point in the creative process, the individual or team has ideally:
- suspended judgment about "the decision,"
- completed step 1 to fully understand the opportunity, identify an initiative goal, and significantly broaden their experience and understanding of variables that can promote or restrain success.
- completed step 2 to develop a commendable junk drawer of a variety of options that they are confident can be combined into a solution to your opportunity statement,
- and is now eager and prepared to make a decision about an alternative which will fulfill the initiative's opportunity statement.

Idea Box

This clever tool allows you to arrange all of your preferred good ideas (written on Post-Its) on one flip chart sheet, and to imagine combinations of the ideas that could assemble into a great solution that fulfills your scoreboard.

1. Select your preferred options from your previous exercises. This is a Post-It shopping spree. Walk along the wall where your brainstorming flip charts are posted, tiers 1 and 2. Pick the Post-Its of the ideas you like. Everyone does this simultaneously.
2. Once all the preferred Post-Its are on one flip chart, silently organize them into groups that belong together.
3. Discuss and title the groups.
4. On another flip chart place a Post-It titled with each of the group titles as row headers.
5. Move the Post-Its from the groups into rows with the appropriate title.
6. Build alternative solutions by linking different options of Post-Its between rows. If two or more items in a row could be used simultaneously, see if the total combination is attractive.
7. Analyze the alternative solutions and select the best one(s). Follow the lines in the diagram below to see which Post-Its assembled represent a possible combination.
8. Confirm assembled solutions are both feasible and fulfill the scoreboard.

Great Family Two Week Vacation

Criteria	Options					
Location	Florida	Bahamas	Colorado	New York	Gulf Shores	Home
Activities	swimming	boating	hiking	fishing	Playing cards	Museums
Lodging	Fancy hotel	Cheap hotel	Home stay	Camping		
Restaurants	mexican	french	american	chinese	Self cooked	
Cost	<$1000	$1000-$2000	$2000-$3000	$3000-$4000		

Vacation # 1: Florida/boating & swimming/camping/self cooked/$1000-$2000

Vacation # 2: Home/playing cards/self cook/home stay/<$1000

Vacation # 3; New York/museums/cheap hotel/ all except self cooked/$3000-$4000

TILMAG

This tool has the advantage of being structured to provoke associations between preferred components of a total solution. Without a tool like this, teams will often assume that varied components of a solution may be contradictory and hence must be compromised to work together. This is very similar to "the hat" in the house of quality from QFD (quality function deployment).

1. State the problem clearly, brainstorm possible solution ideas.
2. Identify and define Identify Ideal Solution Elements (ISEs). Which components of the solution would you like to coordinate and optimize?
3. Construct an association matrix, write the ISEs on each axis (in top row and side column).
4. Brainstorm and record associations for each paired ISE.
5. Transfer the underlying principle of each association back to the problem for possible solutions.
6. Pool the best ideas from both the TILMAG associations and the initial brainstorming session.

TILMAG - Great Company Party Location

	1. Easy access	2. Interesting	3. Affordable	4. Variety
4. variety	-Bus -Car -walk	-Amusement events -Casino theme	-Single vendor -employees create events	X
3. affordable	-Car pool -Public transportation	-Employees host casino games -Employee talent show	X	X
2. interesting	-Hitchhike -Long limo	X	X	X

Prioritizing with Scoreboard, Multivoting, and Decision Matrix

This sequence is one of my favorite sequences of decision-making exercises that promotes and provokes dialogue is Scoreboard, Brainstorm, Multivote and Decision Matrix. You may read the details of this sequence at the end of the Improvement Process Step Five: Practice Process Improvement Skills.

Identify your opportunity statement, scoreboard, and alternatives solutions.

1. Document the alternative solutions you want to consider.
2. Choose your current time frame or other constraints if applicable.
3. Establish or review Scoreboard to assist you in the next steps.

Select the ideas from your alternatives that best fulfill the scoreboard

4. While looking at all the alternatives, and considering your goal criteria, Multivote your list to narrow it down to your top five or six choices.
5. Using these top 5 or 6 choices, and your goal criteria, complete a Decision Matrix
6. Confirm each member supports the decisions these tools assisted you in making.

4. Implement Ideas

As with the improvement teams, I prefer that the team with the great new idea consider how they will transfer their improved process to the group that will be using the new idea in such a way that the new group can and wants to succeed with the new idea.

Remembering that creativity is about generating great new ideas, and that innovation is about turning the ideas into new products, services, and revenues, *implementing* great these new ideas is another topic. There are many excellent books to recommend how to build innovation capability. One of my favorites is *Innovating the Corporation: Creating Value for Customers and Shareholders,* by Thomas D. Kuczmarski, Arthur Middlebrooks, and Jeffrey Swaddling (NTC Business Books, 2001).

7
Additional Ideation Tools and Techniques

Dr. Edward de Bono – Creative Thinking Skills Pioneer

My first introduction to Dr. Edward de Bono was reading *Lateral Thinking* in 1982. Here I learned about the difference between thinking and intelligence and many of his early creative thinking skills techniques.

After I began my consulting business in 1990, I quickly found his training organization and spent my two weeks getting certified in both Six Thinking Hats and Lateral Thinking. I use Dr. de Bono's ideas and approaches in many of my client assignments.

Dr de Bono's work is all over the world and all over the internet. There are thousands of references to both his helpful ideas and the many successes his students have enjoyed. In this chapter I will review my suggestions developed over the past twenty-plus years about some of de Bono's approaches. I do recommend that anyone wanting to use these ideas seriously seek out one of the many resources providing valuable training in the use of Dr. de Bono's ideas. I have seen few groups who have only "read the book" realize the full benefits of his approaches, and end with a short comment by Michael Schrage about

BOPSAT.

Edward de Bono's Six Thinking Hats

One of my favorite thinking processes is Edward de Bono's *Six Thinking Hats*.

De Bono suggests there are six types of thinking that you unconsciously use every day. Each metaphorical hat represents one of those six ways of thinking. A person wearing an imaginary White Hat focuses on factual information, a Yellow Hat on positive perspective, a Black Hat on caution and risk, a Green Hat on creativity, a Red Hat on emotions and intuition, and a Blue Hat on control, overview and organization.

Short descriptions:

- **White Hat:** Neutral and objective — pure facts and figures — what we know and want to know.
- **Yellow Hat:** Optimism, values and benefits — why it will work — symbolizes sunshine, brightness and optimism - positive and constructive
- **Black Hat:** Judgment, devil's advocate — why it will not work — risk assessment — caution, not argument — critical negative judgment
- **Green Hat:** Possibilities, alternatives, and new ideas — symbolizes fertility, growth and the value of creative thinking
- **Red Hat:** Feelings, hunches, intuition — legitimizes emotions and feelings — "This is how I feel."
- **Blue Hat:** Managing the thinking process — the "control hat" — sets the focus — defines the problems and shapes the questions

A complete listing of the hats and their uses is available in de Bono's *Six Thinking Hats or Serious Creativity.*

Starting points – A Tool to Comprehensively Consider an Option

In my experience, Six Hats is a technique best used to help you consider one possible alternative solution at a time. It is not a self-contained meeting process. It is not exclusively a creative thinking process. It is a sequence of six very helpful questions.

Used correctly, the process encourages people to separate fact from opinion, to look fully at both positive and negative opinions and to get hidden agendas that can sabotage any meeting on the table. It stimulates their innate creativity and helps them discover how to turn seemingly insoluble problems into real opportunities.

Used correctly, the hats keep your different kinds of thinking separated, focused and controlled. They enable you to evaluate situations by consciously switching in and out of the six thinking modes (hats). This process teaches an individual to look at decisions and problems systematically.

Each meeting participant uses the same hat color at the same time together. Used correctly, the hats keep your different kinds of thinking separated, focused and controlled. Incorrect use would have each person with their own different color hat sharing their ideas only when their hat is being considered. Using the Six Hats simultaneously is chaos.

Preparing to Use the Six Hats

Like other collaboration tool sessions, a team should

be in a room with table and chairs, and good wall space to post flip chart sheets. Other materials should include Post-Its and possibly a flip chart of the hats and their descriptions posted next to the work area.

I'm a real fan of asking each participant to write their own ideas on Post-It notes, one per Post-It, silently during the data gathering time.

Then, standing at a flip chart titled with the current hat color, use as much time as necessary to debrief each person's ideas so everyone understands everyone else's points of view. Agreement is not required. Treat each hat separately: i.e. hat 1 data gathering/debrief, hat 2 data gathering/debrief, etc.

Here is an example of hat sequence and silent writing and debrief times:

- White: 4 minutes alone then 5-10 minutes team debrief
- Yellow: 4 minutes alone then 5-10 minutes team debrief
- Black: 4 minutes alone then 5-10 minutes team debrief
- Green: 4 minutes alone then 5-10 minutes team debrief
- Red: 30 seconds and very quick debrief
- Blue: 4 minutes alone then 5-10 minutes team debrief

Using the Six Hats with Other Tools

In a complex situation you may not complete all hats in one meeting. In a simple situation, you may complete the whole meeting in less than an hour. You can also use the hats working alone. You can spend more time on a hat if the conversation is not completed. Do gather ideas for each hat at least once during a thinking session.

Here is an example of a use of six hats in a meeting:

1. Consider your issue and identify your goal (opportunity statement).
Example: Reduce the time airline passengers have to wait in ticket lines?

2. Identify your goal's success criteria, your scoreboard:
Example: Passengers will have to wait only 15 minutes or less to process their ticket, seating assignment, and baggage.

3. Identify one alternative solution (from brainstorming for example).
Example: Staff ticket lines with 1 ticket agent for each 5 people in the waiting area.

4. Select and carry out a sequence of the Six Hats.
Considering the selected alternative, what do we know and want to know about it (White Hat); why is it a good idea, as measured by the scoreboard (Yellow Hat), etc.

5. Carry out a sequence of the Six Hats as outlined above on each selected new alternative solution.
If you have three possible alternatives you want to consider, you need to exercise the Six Hats three times.

6. For your final alternative selection, use your preferred convergent tool; decision matrix for example.

Benefits of the Six Hats Include:

- Each Hat asks for one different kind of data, but not the same data or ideas
- Well-prepared participants can complete a quick consideration of many points of view that result from answering the Six Hat questions
- Each participant uses the same hat at the same time diminishing/eliminating the confusion of having different kinds of data being considered at the same time (de Bono's Parallel Thinking)
- The opportunity to develop a common starting point
- Having the team suspend judgment while points of view are being considered

To emphasize just how useful the hats can be, imagine a meeting without the hats. Six to ten people meeting in a room around a table, wanting to move towards a decision, a variety of opinions, agendas, and energies around the table. One person begins and says "Just what do we know about the situation?" (white hat). Immediately someone else adds "We know enough to say it's a really good idea." (yellow hat). Another counters "Good idea, you've got to be kidding." (black hat). From the end of the table comes "You know, this is not the only option we have (green hat). Next we hear "Just does not feel right to me, something's missing." (red hat). And finally, "Where are we on the meeting agenda, what's next?" (blue hat).

This might be considered a normal meeting in many organizations. Some would call it dysfunctional. The point I am trying to make is that without a standard for structure of the different kinds of ideas (Six Hats), all the different ideas (hats) are presenting concurrently, each competing for air time and attention.

The significant benefit of de Bono's hats is that it

structures the same information in a way that it can be both solicited and considered in a sane way. De Bono calls this parallel thinking. And by separating the kinds of ideas and thinking, the team can focus on the goals and supporting ideas with far less competition.

Six Thinking Hats and Decision Making

Many teams have trouble making decisions. Some team members will want to move ahead quickly and force a decision, while some will want to take more time to consider all the data. Six Thinking Hats helps teams work in between these two extremes.

A story often shared in training circles is about five blind people who had never seen an elephant. The five circled the animal and touched it with their hands to gather data. When they shared their findings, the person near the trunk could only describe a long cylindrical object. The one near the feet viewed the elephant as a massive tree trunk. The third, who was at the tail, reported something all together different.

One option for this team would be to argue about their own points of view to confirm their findings. Another would be to accept that, because of their point of view, they were limited in what they could learn from their own vantage point. They could appreciate their circumstantial fallibility and open the conversation to all points of view, working to integrate these points of view into a single comprehensive understanding of the whole elephant.

Six Thinking Hats does a great job of walking a team around their elephant or issue, gathering useful data efficiently, with six points of view, while suspending judgment, promoting team learning, and helping the team to arrive at a common understanding of an issue before they move toward making a decision.

Role of Questions and Additional Collaboration Tools

You may have read earlier in this book, or in my earlier books *Think or Sink* and *Collaborate* about the important role of tools and the questions they ask. To review, good questions answered by a team together help the team learn what they need to know to solve a problem or develop a new solution. They are a key strategy to productive collaboration.

Fundamentally, the Six Hats represents six categories of questions:

- White Hat - What do we know and want to know?
- Yellow Hat - Why might the idea work?
- Black Hat - Why might the idea not work?
- Green Hat - What are some alternatives to the idea?
- Red Hat - What is your intuition about the idea?
- Blue Hat - Knowing what we know now, what should we do next?

Six Hats is particularly effective when combined with other best practice collaboration tools. The other tools complement the categories of questions by asking supporting questions that require additional data and specificity.

Six Thinking Hats – Six Categories of Questions in Advanced Use

Advanced Use - White Hat tips

White Hat: *information known or needed*, neutral and objective, pure facts and figures, imitates the computer, first class facts, checked and proven (*Six Thinking Hats,* pages 25-46).

Many teams will most often start off with the White Hat.

The white hat helps teams:

- develop a common starting point
- identify opposing ideas
- discuss the important details
- help everyone to be heard
- clarify data needs

One White Hat exercise series I have called Big Picture in earlier chapters and *Collaborate* includes the following steps:

1. Develop an opportunity statement: "What is our goal?"
2. Develop a scoreboard for the opportunity statement: success as measured by, better with quantitative goals; three to five items.
3. Develop a large diagram (ex: two flipcharts side-by-side) of the current situation. This should be a very honest picture of the starting point, working hard to identify and include all the variables that contribute to the situation, like an exploded diagram of an object with all the labels of the parts included.

Examples of tools that can help with the White Hat (instructions in this and other *Good Thinking Series* books):

- flow chart
- interrelationship digraph
- relationship diagram
- income statement, balance sheet
- value chain

The point is to build an understanding of the current situation with everyone's points of view. It's often messy and complicated, but it is an excellent paper trail of the team's learning. If people disagree on a point, find the data that clarifies current reality.

Pass the marker around the group so everyone can add their data. Once this is completed the team selects one possible solution that might satisfy the scoreboard and uses the remaining hats to learn how it will fulfill the opportunity statement.

If a team doesn't like any starting solutions, they would move to the green hat next (what are some alternative solutions) and then return to yellow, black, and red.

Advanced Use – Yellow and Black Hat Tips

Yellow Hat: *"Optimism, values and benefits, why it will work* - symbolizes sunshine, brightness and optimism - positive and constructive - probes and explores for value and benefit - strives to find logical support - creates concrete proposals and suggestions - speculative and opportunity seeking - permits visions and dreams." (*Six Thinking Hats*, p.89)

Black Hat: *"Judgment, devil's advocate, why it will not work, risk assessment* - caution, not argument - critical negative judgment - risk analysis - logical reasons must be given - points out dangers and potential problems - points out faults in a design." (*Six Thinking Hats*, p.71)

Both Yellow and Black Hats are most useful when you are comparing your prospective alternative to a scoreboard - success as measured by. Just what do we really want to accomplish? When we have found a solution, what will it fulfill? If possible the scoreboard will include categories and numbers. So "improving quality, cost, and delivery" is better than "improve revenues" and "improving quality to 150 DPM, cost to \$2.50 per item and delivery to one day" are even better. The clearer the finish line, the easier it is for the team to know what they're working towards and to recognize when they're done.

Exercising the Yellow Hat provides an optimistic review of why an alternative might best support the scoreboard. The Black Hat work provides a cautionary review of characteristics of the possible solution that do not support the scoreboard.

To objectively compare the yellow and black hats, have all members for a period of time, say 3-4 minutes, brainstorm and debrief all the possible benefits (Yellow Hat). Then brainstorm and debrief all the possible speed bumps/roadblocks (Black Hat) of an alternative. It's best to present these on a flip chart, and working with Post-Its on a flip chart makes it easier to move them around later. It is important to treat each Hat's work separately - do not move back and forth between hats.

Collecting Yellow Hat and Black Hat ideas from the same person may not be so easy. Done well, each participant steps to the side of their own opinion and for this period time "plays the game" of thinking of possible benefits. So each person will have the chance to provide ideas that do not necessarily represent their own current thinking. The team will decide later if these ideas, or an others, will affect the decision to select a possible solution.

Choosing to use a decision matrix will systematically compare an alternative's contribution to each scoreboard criteria; low contribution scores represent Black Hat, high contribution scores represent Yellow Hat.

A common reaction in many of my training sessions and facilitated meetings comes when we begin to discuss the Black Hat. "Black Hat, oh yeah, that's our boy Bob, or our girl Sally - such incredible naysayers - never have a positive thing to say..."

An earlier quote stated that, "It is a universal truth that those who are not dissatisfied will never make any progress." As Alan Robinson notes in *Continuous Improvement in Operations: A Systematic Approach to Waste Reduction* (Productivity Press, 1991):

> "Yet even if one feels dissatisfaction, it must not be diverted into complaining; it must be actively linked to improvement. In this sense, we can say that dissatisfaction is the mother of improvement. There are many examples of waste in the workplace, but not all waste is obvious. It often appears in the guise of useful work. We must see beneath the surface and grasp the essence. Never being content and always looking for ways to make things better are prime prerequisites for uncovering problems."

One of the drumbeats of the *Good Thinking Series* of books might be "Conflict is synonymous with options. Resolving options is much more fun than resolving conflict; the big difference is how you think about it." So in the case of the Black Hat thinker, first appreciate they are not Black Hat people. They might exercise the Black Hat more often than others, but we can learn to leverage their point of view. Here's how. Don't let the Black Hat list be an endpoint. List their and others' Black Hat ideas. Then prioritize them by impact against the scoreboard. Then wonder out loud how you could reduce or eliminate their effect. Doing this lets the team fully consider the forces that will resist their success. By targeting and working them out on the table, they become strategies to improve the success of the alternative.

Examples of additional supporting tools (instructions in this and other *Good Thinking Series* books):

- Force Field diagram
- Business Environment Analysis

Advanced Use - Green Hat Tips

Green Hat: advanced creative thinking skills.

De Bono's Green Hat is a study all its own. It is synonymous with creativity, which de Bono entitles lateral thinking. I learned this first from de Bono's 1970 book Lateral Thinking, and later during my instructor certification week with de Bono in 1993.

De Bono's Lateral thinking techniques are great precipitating events (chapter five). An introduction to Lateral Thinking-type thinking is included in chapter six, especially tier two tools.

The Oxford Dictionary lists lateral thinking as "a way of thinking that seeks solutions to intractable problems through unorthodox methods or elements that would normally be ignored by logical thinking." de Bono's original example on an early radio program in the 1960s compared digging deeper for a solution vs. stepping to the side (laterally) to dig in another spot seeking the same target. de Bono appreciates how the brain works in trying to solve problems and summarized his work this way: "In self organizing information systems, patterns (new concepts formed in the brain) are formed. Lateral thinking is a method for cutting across patterns. It is for changing concepts and perceptions." de Bono helps students learn that breakthrough ideas do not have to be a shotgun effort. His tools provide a deliberate, systematic process that will result in more innovative thinking.

Some of De Bono's Lateral Thinking tools are:

- Alternatives: sometimes we do not look beyond the obvious alternatives. Sometimes we do not look for alternatives at all. This session shows how to extract the concept behind a group of alternatives and then use it to generate further alternatives.
- Challenge: what is out there, what is our current thinking — not an attack or criticism or attempt to show why something is inadequate — a challenge to uniqueness — what might be a better way.
- Random input: quickest and simplest lateral thinking technique - useful for creating ideas for new products or service. If you start from a different point, then you increase the likelihood of opening up patterns different from those you would have used.
- Provocation: cut across from the main track to a side track by using a stepping stone - something that is obvious in hindsight may be invisible to foresight.
- Harvesting: deliberate attempt to gather up, pull in all the creative value that has emerged during a creative thinking effort.

This book's chapter six include complementary alternatives to de Bono's lateral thinking tools. To learn more, see de Bono's *Lateral Thinking* or *Serious Creativity*.

Advanced Use - Red Hat Tips

Red Hat - *Feelings, hunches, intuition - legitimizes emotions and feelings*

"This is how I feel - fears, dislikes, loves, hates - the opposite of neutral, objective information - keep it short - no need to give reasons for the basis - allows exploring the feelings of others." (*Six Thinking Hats,* p.47-70)

When exercising Six Hats in a sequence, I most often use the Red Hat after White, Yellow, Black, and Green to help the team consider what they've learned in the previous conversations and how it all feels going forward. I find a discussion of the Red Hat data often generates a variety of useful points of view and questions that improves the quality of the previous Hats' listings.

While I most often allow 3-5 minutes for the first four hats, the Red Hat data should be initially solicited and shared within thirty seconds - no long explanations, rationalizations, apologies, or confessions.

The information shared during a Red Hat review provides a wonderful opportunity to consider information participants may have which they cannot readily either describe easily, fit into another hat, or explain its source. Some will call it "from the gut", others will call it "my intuitive voice". So whether you call it your special friend or Jiminy Cricket, I encourage you to include the Red Hat data as you move ahead to decide on a particular alternative whether it's a car, a house, a bar, or a spouse.

As an engineering manager at Intel many years ago, I developed an approach I called "first voice." This referred to my stomach knotting up a bit if a person in my group behaved in a way that wasn't aligned with their tasks or our goals. I learned to listen for and respond to this signal and quickly, within a day, would sit down with the individual and talk about what I saw, its' impact, and ask for their thinking about the situation. I think now it is a required skill for leaders who help employees by holding them accountable. And this is not to micromanage or carry a big stick. It's just to initiate the conversation about what helps and doesn't help in a productive work setting. The much less preferred alternative would be to notice the behavior, assume it will get better on its own, and let it slide.

As a very amateur golfer, I have come to step back and notice how I prefer to putt when I finally get to the green. I do not spend a lot of time checking the profiles by dropping to my knee, or walking around the ball to catch all the details about relative ups and downs of the grass. I do however line up my line of sight so I can see the entire view of the ball all the way to the pin. I settle for a second or two, putt, and at least occasionally surprise my fellow golfers with some very long putts. It's sort of like "One side John, we'll take care of this..." and whatever intuitive athletic ability I might drum up comes to play without me thinking a lot about it...at least to my knowledge.

Rumor has it that Richard Feynman (PhD, Cal Tec; Manhattan Project, Quantum Physics whiz, Space Shuttle Disaster detective, etc; *So What Do You Care What Other People Think,* and *Surely You're Joking Mr. Feynman*), as a young student who had aced most college entrance tests, could not decide to attend MIT or CIT. He finally chose to let the decision rest on a coin toss. He tossed and the coin came up "MIT," to which he responded "No way..." and subsequently attended CIT to begin his spectacular career.

I saw my oldest daughter do the same thing as she tried to decide where to go to college. She sat across me at the breakfast nook, wrote a carefully worded acceptance letter to one school, read it carefully, and tore it up. "Just doesn't feel right." She accepted elsewhere and enjoyed it very much.

There are numerous examples in a wide variety of

books. Jerry B. Harvey's The Abilene Paradox and other Meditations on Management (also a great 30 minute video/DVD, and mentioned again later in this chapter) helps readers appreciate the value of listening to one's own voice, expressing it without fear, and often learning much to their surprise they actually were representing the majority of the team when they thought they were the odd-man out.

And finally, Malcolm Gladwell's *Blink: The Power of Thinking Without Thinking* provides a number of examples of where "the power of the trained mind to make split second decisions, the ability to think without thinking" has served individuals and teams well.

A productive use of the Red Hat does not promote SWAG (silly wild alternative guess, etc.) decision making. Listening for and to "your heart", "first voice" or intuition can at least alert you to a point of view, information, a question, etc that can lead you to a more useful line of thinking and decision making.

Examples of additional supporting tools (instructions in this and other *Good Thinking Series* books): And On Cups.

Advanced Use - Blue Hat tips

Blue Hat: managing the thinking process - the "control hat" - the orchestra conductor - organized the thinking (Six Thinking Hats p.145)

Nothing happens in hockey until the puck is dropped. Nothing happens in organizations until decisions are made. Knowing what we know now, what should we do next? In my experience the most important part of this phrase is "do".

A company's success is basically the result of the number of great decisions implemented successfully, at a minimum cost. This implies that it is optimal to have all employees make the decisions appropriate for them. Minimize/eliminate micromanaging. Some call this empowerment. Benchmarking successful companies would reveal leadership's role in authoring and proliferating great processes that support great decision making. The feedback from the processes informs the employees and leadership if/that the processes are doing what was intended or that something needs attention way before any defects are generated. The purpose of the blue hat is to help the team discuss and plan its next steps forward. Many planning tools can help here.

Examples of additional supporting tools (instructions in this and other *Good Thinking Series* books):

- Strategic Planning
- Scenario Planning
- Systematic Diagram
- Process Decision Program Chart
- Gantt Chart
- Impact/Ease Diagram
- Interrelationship Digraph.

Six Thinking Hats – Common Misuses

I often see untrained teams assigning one hat color to one person and asking that person to represent that hat concurrently with the other hats. Here each hat does get represented but it does lend itself to a argument among the six hats. The purpose of the hat color is to solicit those types of ideas, one type at a time. You know this may happen when you see their meeting room with one hat of each color for a total of six. If a team was going to invest in hats, they would need each color hat (6) for each team member. In use each team member wears the same color hat at the same time.

I see untrained teams using the hats to provide them an opportunity to present their opinion. The yellow hat people go first, then the black hat people, etc. So the hats are separated, but this lends itself to having people associate themselves and their opinions with one color and wait till their color is requested. The purpose of the hat color is to solicit those types of ideas, one type at a time; ideas, not just opinions. One way to set up the sequence to avoid this inclination is to say, "If someone (not just you) really liked this idea (yellow hat) what would they be thinking and writing on their post its?" "If someone (not just you) really did not like this idea (black hat) what would they be thinking and writing on their post its?" Here I am working hard to get all the ideas possible for each hat so they are available to the whole team to consider (junk drawer).

I see untrained teams trying to assign a hat color to a personality. "Oh, Bob is so black hat, such a naysayer." While people may have tendencies personally, they likely exercise all six types of ideas during their workdays. The effective use of the hats focuses on using the hats to solicit lots of ideas in all the colors.

Another Valuable de Bono Idea: PO

Edward de Bono's website (www.edwdebono.com) reports the following:

- NO is the basic tool of the Logic System.
- YES is the basic tool of the Belief System.
- PO is the basic tool of the Creative System.

"PO is a device for changing our ways of thinking: a method for approaching problems in a new and more creative way. It is the product of a research scientist who notably - and very entertainingly - thinks for himself. PO is a new thinking tool - but with a completely different function. PO lets you step outside the harsh rigidity of the YES/NO system and change from the present thought pattern to creating new ideas "

Abilene Paradox

Some of you likely have seen the classic training video Abilene Paradox (Jeffrey Harvey) – a wonderful introduction to the social phenomenon (predictable, like rip currents) of team members guessing what the team wants, saying they want that too so they will be seen as a team player, while the whole team actually does not want to do the something in question—lemmings to the sea. That's right, sometimes teams guess what the team wants but everyone gets it exactly wrong. Watching the video establishes a spectacular metaphor for the team: Don't go to Abilene, i.e. tell me what you really think or know, and let's deal with that rather than your politically correct statement. Teams going to Abilene are like teams swimming against rip currents. If they knew more about how tides or teams worked, they would be able to choose a more productive course of action.

Abilene – PO to the Rescue

Collaboration skills, a significant theme of the *Good Thinking Series*, help teams to cope with potential team dysfunctions like the Abilene Paradox, or teams unable to discuss controversial topics. This of course is disappointing, socially and financially, because the reason they are controversial is that they are important to the players, that's why they're pushing back.

PO is only a word but used correctly can help a team stay out of the rip currents of the Abilene Paradox and other counterproductive team behavior options. For example a team is heading to Abilene by saying, "Yes, we all should move to Cincinnati now for lots of good reasons..." But out in the hallway and over beers other conversations talk about the many valid reasons why it may not be a very good idea, at least right now, Housing prices here are too low to sell well, or volume is so low we'll have little to do at the new facility, etc etc."

So at a next meeting, a brave team member listens for a while to the "let's move now" arguments, pauses and says "PO." At this point, a trained team would know to stop the train of conversation, know that the announcer has something different and important to say, and listens, doing their best to put the team opinion to the side for a minute and consider another idea objectively.

So, "PO, I don't think everyone really wants to move right now. I want to hear from each team member here and now about how they really think and feel about moving. Tell us your truth. Let's put all the options out on the table" This introduction would hopefully generate a very useful conversation among the decision makers about some very real options.

Airline Pilot Teams Going to Abilene

Malcolm Gladwell's book, *Outliers*, shares some pretty scary stories about true airline cockpit conversations where PO wasn't used. Pilot, co-pilot, and flight engineer teams talked around some very real issues (actual location of the plane in Guam, and the actual level of fuel circling JFK), and both planes crashed without the benefit of a healthy, robust dialogue about all the data that was available from the three cockpit team members.

In the case of a different thinker, Chesley "Sully" Sullenberger "Miracle on the Hudson." (US Airways flight 1549) asked his crew as they headed for the Hudson "got any ideas?" This is PO in action. This is also in many cases asking for a person's Red Hat, unvarnished.

Stamp out BOPSAT - Collaboration and Shared Space

The more I facilitate working sessions, the more I notice how taking the time to set up the work area and supporting processes (collaboration tools), the bigger difference it makes in the efficiency and productivity of the meeting.

As with other collaboration tools, using the wall, posting data on flip charts creates common work space while reducing eye contact which often contributes to unnecessary escalating interpersonal conflicts. Using the wall focuses the team on the goals and ideas. Having people only sit around a table allows the team to regress to personal agendas and strong opinions.

In an online article on the subject, from *Intellimeet* (http://gointellimeet.com/blog/?m=201004), Michael Schrage, research fellow at the Massachusetts Institute of Technology and author of two critically-acclaimed books about collaboration, states that collaboration requires shared space, that collaborative thinking requires a space —be it a napkin, flip chart, whiteboard, or some other medium—where the collaborators are able to share their thoughts.

"Why does collaboration require shared space? ... Imagine a meeting of a dozen people in an office conference room. They are seated around a boardroom table. The group's meeting method is what I like to call the

BOPSAT—Bunch Of People Sitting Around Talking."

More precisely, people take turns talking. As Schrage describes it, "When someone talks, he is the focus of discussion. People look at him. People react to what he says and how he looks...The meeting is a carousel of egos, each grasping for the brass ring of attention. The group does nothing." He goes on to explain that the group does nothing because, "Everything about the design of the meeting encourages individuals to make their points, not the group to create a shared understanding. . . . There's nothing in the ecology of meetings that encourages collaborative creativity, problem solving, or decision making."

"What's missing from the ecology of a BOPSAT meeting is shared space. Have you ever noticed how the character of a meeting changes when someone gets up and starts recording ideas on a whiteboard or flip chart? Everyone turns to face the shared space. People contribute their ideas to it. The combination of ideas begins to take shape. As Schrage explains, "The key is to create an environment that shifts attention away from the individual participant and toward community expression.

"The key element, the key ingredient, the key medium for successful and effective collaboration is the creation and maintenance of shared space. You cannot create shared understandings without shared space."

And someone needs to stand up literally and have the courage to change the arrangement of the workspace to take advantage of this significant insight.

Additional Resources

There are likely hundreds of books about problem solving, process improvement, and creative thinking. I encourage you to pursue the best combination of resources, and tools and techniques, that serve you best. Like a great buffet table, take what you will use. Don't try to learn it all before you begin to practice. The practice and the improved results will motivate and direct you to your next best tool and technique. In searching for other resources do consider that you are hunting for better questions. The questions are the change agent that provokes new thinking and resulting insights.

8
Prepare to Implement this New Thinking

"Every time a person puts a new idea across, they face a dozen people who thought of it before they did. But they only thought of it."

—Oren Arnold

One Thing That Will Remain the Same: Change Will Continue to Occur

As it's been said, "The future's not what it used to be." We experience change every day. In business, in our communities, in our homes, in our churches. Often change has a bad rap. We are creatures of comfort and don't mind things staying the same for a while so we can enjoy the good times, enjoy a rest, not have to think about it.

Competitiveness Requires Change

We live in a competitive world. Commerce is now global and for us to succeed we must be able to compete with, better exceed, our competition in providing products and services to our global markets. To compete, we must improve. To improve we must change. To change we must start doing something new, and stop what we have been doing that doesn't help anymore. One way to think about this has us deliberately substituting "improvement" for "change" at every chance. When we can operationalize improvement (change), when we can improve first and faster that our competitors, then we are acting proactively to secure our future.

Successful Change Strategies - Characteristics

What does it take to change a habit? Perhaps you have tried to change on a personal basis, whether your goal was to read more, weigh less, exercise more, or sleep less. Thinking back, just how successful have you or a loved one been in actually achieving the target? Successful goal achievers often report a laser beam focus on their goal, a discipline and schedule to the work to achieve it, honest feedback and encouragement, and a celebration of the new process that supports maintaining the goal. This is basic human nature stuff. People can change.

So now apply this to your organization:

- Can you think of anyone who hasn't attained their goal without deliberate effort? Do you know any organization that has improved accidently?
- Does your organization have a short list of key goals (to honor the Pareto Principle: the vital few and trivial many)?
- Does your organization have disciplined and structured support to guide this change (Change Agent Skills delivered on an ongoing basis to your employees/leaders responsible for influencing others)?
- Does your organization review feedback objectively in a regular basis to assess progress?

- Does your organization celebrate your wins on a regular basis? Are you changing and improving deliberately faster than your competitors?
- Are you satisfied with your process and results?

Successful Change Strategies - Assess Your Starting Point

All too often companies are pretty good at identifying ideas to improve and innovate but weak on the implementation and delivery. Good ideas get tackled by fear, pessimism, inertia, and politics. In my experience, what is needed is a special team of employees/leaders who are responsible for moving the ideas through the implementation stages. Many call these people change agents. Good change agents help teams make better decisions that more team members support.

Is your organization staffed with capable change agents? Can your teams make and implement great decisions faster than your competitors?

What a wonderful opportunity—to *not* copy your competitors who will "save money" by not continuing to develop their change capability—especially in tough economic times. One company hunkers down and weathers the storm. The other works through the rain and wind. Which company would you bet on when times get good again? It really depends on whether you see employee skills development as a cost or investment.

So What

Leaders who proactively learn about how things happen in teams, like considering options and making decisions, are better prepared to help their teams make great decisions everyone supports. Good decisions with good support is good business.

One of my primary insights after ten years in industry, (Intel and Herman Miller) and twenty years as an independent consultant around the world, is that thinking drives performance. Consider:

- Improved performance is the result of improved behaviors and decisions.
- Improved behaviors and decisions are the result of improved ideas.
- Improved ideas—breadth, depth, content, etc.—are the result of better thinking.

If this is close to true, considering the thinking that a leader uses is considering the DNA of their leadership and its effect on an organization. You could target behaviors and ask the suspect not to use them, but if you haven't provided an opportunity for the suspect to select new thinking, their behavior is likely to stay the same.

So, just how serious is an organization that says it really wants to be profitable, and a great place to work, but doesn't want to or cannot talk about the real source of the behavior? These nasty, unproductive behaviors are likely present in an organization that describes itself at the water cooler as dysfunctional. These nasty, unproductive behaviors are sources of waste right along the lines of Taiichi Ohno's famous seven sources of waste. So, it's OK in some companies to actively and deliberately pursue factory and process waste, but not OK to talk about waste-behaviors. Considering the enormous cost of dysfunction, this may be the next organizational performance frontier.

The chart below sort of captures my thinking about this performance and thinking link across a range of possible individuals. Read in columns:

Canfield's Attitude Matrix

PERCEPTION OF THE SAME SITUATION				
THINKING	Mess	Problem	Change	Improvement	Competitive Opportunity
PERCEPTION OF ROLE				
IDEAS	Victim	Attendee	Participant	Contributor	Owner
PERCEPTION OF RESPONSIBILITY				
BEHAVIOR	Blame	Wait	Manage	Proactive Do	Lead
BOTTOM LINE				
RESULTS	Awful	Ho Hum	Good	Better	Best

First of all, please notice the setting: the five individuals (columns) shown above are all sitting in the same situation. Yet their perceptions are significantly different.

The person in the first column sees a mess and considers themselves a victim ("My bad luck"). He or she reacts by blaming situations and others, and not surprisingly generates awful results.

The person on the other end, in the same situation, sees the light at the end of the tunnel. They lean into the opportunity, own the situation, lead their team, and likely generate admirable results.

In order for you to help build support for improvements, your thinking has to be in a good place. Considering the matrix above, where are you on an issue as you begin to influence others? What's the best way to think about this change issue in order to generate the behaviors in you that you need to support it? If you're not where you want to be, how can you get the information you need to be where you'd prefer to be?

My thirty years of industrial experience says that this is neither naïve nor simplistic. It is fundamental and comprehensive. Improve your thinking, improve your performance. And to my point of view, the column a person operates in is directly related to how they choose to think.

9
Next Steps

The *Good Thinking Series* of books is based upon the notion that improving thinking skills is the key driver to improving business performance. Thinking and intelligence are different. Intelligence is innate capability, and thinking is how you use it. As a skill it is improvable. What differentiates great and not-so-great companies is how they think, and how they help all their employees learn to think more effectively.

Improved Business Performance

↑ **Implementation Skills**

Improved Decisions, Behaviors

↑ **Collaboration Skills**

Improved Insights and Ideas

↑ **Idea Generating Skills**

Improved Thinking

Idea Generating Skills

All of these approaches/skills are supported by a wide variety of tools that guide a person or a team's thinking for a period of time to help generate better ideas. The tools don't tell you what to think, they tell you how so you can come up with more of your ideas that you like.

	Tactical	Strategic
Improve (Convergent)	Process Improvement Skills	Strategic Planning
	Collaboration Skills	
Innovate (Divergent)	Creative Thinking Skills	Scenario Planning

Core Topic: Collaboration Skills

Collaboration can be so much more than just assembling as a team to do work. Done poorly, the results are half-baked ideas sort-of supported by some of the team's members. Done well, the results are decisions that are better than anyone expected, supported enthusiastically by all of a team's members.

Productive collaboration includes the presentation of different points of view, and substantiation with data when possible. There are both ordinary and not-so-ordinary techniques and approaches which generate a wide variety of alternatives while deliberately building support for those alternatives. Effective techniques allow the team to physically place the issue out in front of the group, while minimizing distracting personality issues. Effective tools help teams build and support great decisions. Effective techniques promote better alternatives, better support, and better results.

Collaboration is the key skill set that drives effective teams to improve business performance. Supporting skills sets include idea generating, decision making, and implementing:

- **Process Improvement** targets waste, the 10-30% of a company's revenues most often being spent on unnecessary process steps by companies who have not learned to improve deliberately. Six Sigma and Lean are example methodologies developed to support these efforts. My comments have targeted those who are just starting.
- **Creative Thinking Skills** includes a wide variety of techniques to help individuals and teams to generate/provoke new ideas when they thought they may have had none.
- **Strategic Planning** helps teams develop an operational planning document that guides company leaders and employees, and improves the executive team's ability to identify, prioritize, and assign opportunities.
- **Scenario Planning** helps teams consider alternative futures. The value of this technique comes from the deep dialogue that the different scenario stories provoke. The alternate views generate new insights about a company and their future. Thinking this way helps prepare the contributors to notice and consider emerging ideas before others even perceive any change.

The tools that support these titles promote and provoke dialogue, a conversation that generates learning.

Productive dialogue requires the presentation of different points of view and substantiation with data when possible. Tools allow the team to physically place the issue out in front of the group, while minimizing distracting personality issues.

Added Benefits of Correct Use

What's really neat about the tools is when they are used correctly, they help a team avoid some nasty and money-wasting behaviors while they build both effective decisions and cooperative support simultaneously.

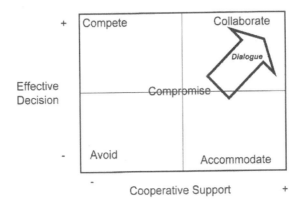

I define collaboration as the successful development of great decisions with great support.

Luck would have it that people behave in a variety of ways. A few behaviors restrain collaboration:

- Avoiders don't really want to help and have few good ideas. They often say, "I really can't help now, sorry."
- Accommodators are just in it for the fun of being together with others. When it's time to make a decision they say, "Whatever you say."
- The compromisers haven't learned to expect more. They settle for half a good decision and half the buy-in that might be developed. Their motto is, "I can live with that."
- The competers would rather do all this themselves. Their mantra is, "My way or the highway."

Our goal, collaborating, is different. Collaborating is all about learning a better way with a group. When these folks have two options, they've learned the best is always the third. Collaborating is a key business communication strategy to both improve and innovate. Settling for less than collaboration is a business decision, and often not a very good one. Using appropriate tools correctly tends to pull groups up into the collaborating corner.

The *Good Thinking Series* of books help you learn how to lead your teams into the upper right corner of collaboration by asking great questions that help teams learn how to handle their tasks in the areas of process improvement, creative thinking skills, strategic planning, and scenario planning.

Implementation Skills

Implementation skills provide the skills to support the implementation of great ideas.

	Current Projects	New Projects
One Project	Project Management	Leading Change
	Collaboration Skills	
Multiple Projects	Leading Teams	Leading an Innovative Organization

There are many good books available to support these topics.

My Favorites:

- **Project Management:** *Project Management Memory Jogger: A Pocket Guide for Project Teams,* Paula Martin and Karen Tate (Goal/QPC, 1997.)

- **Leading Teams:** *The Team Handbook: Second Edition,* Peter Scholtes, Brian Joiner, Barbara Streibel (Joiner Associates, 1996); *The Team Handbook: Third Edition,* Peter Scholtes, Brian Joiner, Barbara Streibel (Joiner Associates, 2003)

- **Leading Change:** *Leading Change,* John P. Kotter, (The Free Press, 1996).

- **Leading an Innovative Organization:** *Innovating the Corporation: Creating Value for Customers and Shareholders,* Thomas D. Kuczmarski, Arthur Middlebrooks, Jeffrey Swaddling, (NTC Business Books, 2001).

Next Steps - Select an Improvement Goal and Strategy

- Select a business goal that needs attention.
- Identify the behaviors, decisions, and ideas that you would prefer to see.
- What thinking approach and style would produce the preferred ideas, behaviors and decisions that would deliver the business goal you seek?
- Then find a resource to help you learn to think that way.

About the Author

John Canfield is an experienced business executive and coach who has been trained to facilitate a wide variety of planning, improvement, and innovation processes. John has many years of experience working and consulting in a wide variety of organizations around the world.

John has earned a B.S. in Mechanical & Industrial Engineering from the University of Minnesota and a B.A. in Political Science and Psychology from Williams College.

Prior to 1990 John was a Senior Engineering Manager for Intel Corporation and later Director of Corporate Quality and Design Research for Herman Miller.

To learn more about John please visit

Website: *www.johncanfield.com*

Article Series: *www.mibiz.com/goodthinking.html*

Videos: *www.youtube.com/canfieldgoodthinking*

LinkedIn: *www.linkedin.com/in/johncanfield*

• • •

Greg Smith is a writer, designer, and teacher. He collaborates on a variety of projects, in a wide-range of genres.

To learn more about Greg, please visit:

www.smithgreg.com

Made in the USA
San Bernardino, CA
23 April 2014